ENDORSEMENTS

Cindy Jacobs has brought forth the research and revelation to bring reformation to the church. *Invading the Enemy's Strongholds* gives divine directives for the church to fulfill Christ's command for us to pray and work for His kingdom to be demonstrated in every nation and His will to be done on earth as it is in heaven.

Dr. Bill Hamon
Bishop of Christian International Ministries
Network (CIMN)
Author of *Day of the Saints*

Reformation means to bring change. For the Church to bring change, we must first endure change. Cindy Jacobs paints a hopeful, encouraging picture of the reformation process God is doing in His Church, so that we can become His vehicle of transformation in the earth. Thank you, Cindy, for this prophetically inspired charge!

Jane Hamon
Apostle, Vision Church @ Christian
International
Author of *Dreams and Visions, The Deborah
Company, The Cyrus Decree, Discernment
and Declarations for Breakthrough*

In this world, there are many people who make an impact on those around them. Then there are others who also make an imprint. But there are only a few who, in addition to impacting and leaving an imprint, blaze a trail that leads multitudes to their destiny. Cindy Jacobs is a true gift from God and this book is a compelling manifesto that will envision, enlighten, and empower you to follow that trail. Read, be blessed, and go change the world!

DR. ED SILVOSO
Author, *Ekklesia: Rediscovering God's Instrument for Global Transformation*
Founder, Transform Our World

The message that Cindy Jacobs imparts through *Invading the Enemy's Strongholds* couldn't be more relevant to the times we are living in. It is a word for this generation. This book will embolden you to be a change agent for the Kingdom of God as you pursue reformation in your sphere of influence.

DR. CHÉ AHN
President, Harvest International Ministry
Senior Pastor, Harvest Rock Church
Pasadena, California
International Chancellor, Wagner University
Founder, Ché Ahn Media

In the middle of Babylonian anti-God culture, the Lord raised up a reformer named Daniel who shook the whole system. Cindy Jacobs' book will give context and strategy to a last-days reformation reality, where in every place, there will be testimonies of God's dominion and rule. With the authority of an outrageous life testimony, my spiritual mother leaves no room for the counsel of despair, nor the escapist abdication of history. Jesus is the Lord of history, and only the one who believes that statement will be able to become a reformer.

Lou Engle

Finally, more than a despairing assessment of eroding social and moral conditions! Cindy found the mind of God in a strategic plan that directs the body of Christ in practical considerations that will return our nation and the nations of the world to hope.

Jim Hennesy
Pastor, Trinity Ministries
Cedar Hill, Texas

INVADING
THE ENEMY'S
STRONGHOLDS

INVADING THE ENEMY'S STRONGHOLDS

TARGETED INTERCESSION THAT UNLEASHES
REVIVAL, AWAKENING, AND REFORMATION

CINDY
JACOBS

DESTINY IMAGE® PUBLISHERS, INC.

P.O. Box 310, Shippensburg, PA 17257-0310

"Publishing cutting-edge prophetic resources to supernaturally empower the body of Christ"

This book and all other Destiny Image and Destiny Image Fiction books are available at Christian bookstores and distributors worldwide.

For more information on foreign distributors, call 717-532-3040.

Reach us on the Internet: www.destinyimage.com.

ISBN 13 TP: 978-0-7684-7591-3
ISBN 13 eBook: 978-0-7684-7592-0

For Worldwide Distribution, Printed in the U.S.A.
1 2 3 4 5 6 7 8 / 28 27 26 25 24

CONTENTS

PART ONE

INVADING ENEMY STRONGHOLDS

CHAPTER 1

THE PRECURSORS
OF REVIVAL

WE ARE SEEING the beginning of great moves across the earth today. Prophets are prophesying revivals and awakenings. The Lord is raising up a new breed of passionate leaders who are hungry for souls. There are 24/7 prayer movements springing up on university campuses, and the fires of the precursors of revival are burning brightly in all-night prayer meetings.

I know that God is raising up great end-time revivalists. Prayer expeditions are being formed into the unreached parts of the earth. To me, there is no doubt that we are moving toward the return of the Lord. There are millions who still need to be saved, and I am crying out to the Lord for laborers to be sent into the harvest fields of the nations.

Why did I spend years of my life writing the book you are about to read? Because we need both revival and reformation. The Bible delivers a clarion call in the Great Commission to go and disciple and teach nations—which includes invading the enemy's strongholds with His Word and targeted intercession.

Once we lead people to Christ, what then? After extensive study and prayer on this subject, I now understand that we are not only meant to make disciples of individuals, but, like the Great Commission says, we are to make disciples of our nations.

Now, that is a big thought! We are to disciple people and train them to not only live good Christian lives but to be God's change agents on earth. This means we are to go back to the beginning of the Book and take back our original creation mandate.

I have preached for 45-plus years. More, if you count the times I taught Sunday school while my parents planted churches. I have been involved in revivals in Argentina, Brazil, Colombia, and other nations. I love revival! Even as I am writing this first chapter, pictures are flashing across my mind of the miracles I have seen—blind eyes opened and deaf ears opened supernaturally. I plan to see many, many more of those powerful sights! I love to preach in stadiums and see hundreds flood the altars.

However, after the lights go out and people have gone home, I have watched once-bright lights for the gospel dim. The very people who came to Christ supernaturally in those revivals now suffer challenges as their governments become oppressive. Even my nation, the United States that I love so much, has now become what many call a post-Christian nation.

Does that mean that I do not believe a massive revival and awakening is coming to America or other nations? Of course not! It will happen. I just know this army of the Lord must be taught to be reformers as well as revivalists. Can we dream one step beyond that to the transformation of our nations?

The Bible is the "how-to" manual to transform the nations. In order to get to that point, we need to learn how to be reformers and understand the biblical worldview. To fulfill our commission to teach nations, we must learn how.

This is a book of the "how-tos." We must study to show ourselves approved unto God. I invite you to really study this book. I believe that you are hungry for both revival and reformation. I long for you to not only read God's Word but learn to read God's world in the light of His Word.

Reformers throughout the centuries have been imprisoned, martyred, persecuted, and mocked, and yet kept going. They righted great wrongs, such as slavery and the right to vote for women. People have marched against injustice and stood against Jim Crow laws and racism.

We stand upon their shoulders. How can we fail to take the batons passed to us in our generation that have often fallen from lifeless hands?

Not on our watch!

WHY A NEW REFORMATION?

As you read through the pages of this book, it is a fair question to ask, "Why do we need a new reformation?" Is this book about the reformation that began in the year 1517 when Martin Luther nailed his Ninety-Five Theses to the door of the Castle Church in Wittenberg, Germany?

Ironically, these "Theses" were not an attack on the church but a re-introduction of true repentance and a call to return to it. At that time, people were paying for indulgences, and, for the most part, justification by faith was not being taught, nor was it understood. Forgiveness of sin was a money-making venture. I believe the Catholic Church today knows we need to be justified by faith.

Martin Luther was not looking to leave the Catholic Church but to reform it. From my study of church history, he did not know the ramifications of his postings as his hammer fell. This is often the case with reformers. You are reading this book because you are at least curious about being a reformer, or you have heard others talk about going from revival to reformation. The generations of God's people have always been called to embody reformation. We either haven't known how or we were, at times, clueless that the Great Commission was much broader than saving souls. It was also about discipling nations.

Jesus's first sermon was clearly much broader than saving souls. He preached:

> *The Spirit of the Lord is upon Me, because He has anointed Me to preach the gospel to the poor; He has sent Me to heal the brokenhearted, to proclaim liberty to the captives and recovery of sight to the blind, to set at liberty those who are oppressed* (Luke 4:18 NKJV).

You might further ask yourself, "What does reformation have to do with me? Why can't we just have revival?" One only has to search the history of past revivals to see revival is the starting place for us on earth. Beyond that point, we need to be the hands and feet to see His will be done "on earth as it is in heaven."

REFLECTIONS ON THE PRECURSORS OF REVIVAL

As we look around the world today, there are revival "rumblings" taking place. We have prayed many years for revival. However, as we see in this season, we must take steps to target our prayers not only toward revival, but what comes as a fruit of revival, and see it maintained. We must, as believers, and certainly as intercessors, see our need to understand that the Creator wants to see individuals revived and nations reformed and restored to biblical understanding and worldview.

When we talk about invading the enemy's strongholds, we must know what those strongholds are and how to recognize them! This involves, as you will learn in the following pages, study, and the development of strategies. We cannot wait until the revivals are upon us to begin our intercession.

There are many strongholds that have been in place in various sectors of society, in some cases, for centuries! We can bemoan them all we want, but that will never change things until we look at the iniquitous roots of how they have grown.

Many nations have known revivals, only to be captured under far-left socialism. Satan continues to work on the big picture of nations while we are busy in the church. Even though we are on fire and busy with the saving of souls, we must ever understand that both revival and reformation need to take place hand-in-hand.

Let me give you one example of our lack of understanding in the US and the effects on our nation when we are mainly caught up in revival without "minding the store," so to speak, of the nation.

During the 1960s, we experienced a great revival called the Jesus People Movement. Yet, during the same time period, prayer and Bible reading were taken out of school. We must learn to both pray and act— to become "prayer activists." We must watch over our nations long before satan throws his strategies into action.

Our good friend, David Barton, studied the effects of prayer being taken out of public schools and found the great problem at that time was children shooting spit wads at each other. (Shooting a piece of wadded-up wet paper through a straw as a projectile.)

Now, our problems are children bringing guns to school and killing each other! The prayers of millions of schoolchildren and reading the Bible in class kept moral ethics in our classrooms.

Let's pray:

> *Father God, awaken us to be watchmen on the walls for our nations and societies.*
> *In Jesus's name.*
> *Amen.*

CHAPTER 2

INFORMED REFORMERS

LOOKING BACK AT the history of civilization, there have been terrible atrocities, and some of them were done in the "name" or guise of Christianity. For instance, the belt buckles for the German Navy and Luftwaffe read, Gott Mit Uns, or "God with us." The Spanish Inquisition (1478-1834) was ostensibly formed to purge heresy from the nation. Among other things, it led to the expulsion of the Jews from Spain in 1492, following the Alhambra Decree. Between 40,000 and 100,000 Sephardic Jews were expelled during that time.[1]

Persecution of Christians around the world is on the rise today. As of March 17, 2023, 360 million Christians face persecution and discrimination for their faith. According to Open Doors, Christianity remains as one of the most persecuted faiths in the world.[2] The North Korean government tops the list of nations for their horrendous acts toward Christians.

Our societies in the United States and around the world badly need reforming. We are called to be salt and light to the world. That begs the question I feel I must ask as an American, "Why is America sliding so quickly into an anti-God society?" Many Christian leaders today are proclaiming, "We need both revival and reformation." Others are teaching about entering into every aspect of society as believers to bring the gospel. It is my opinion that my friend, Lance Wallnau, will be remembered as the modern-day voice for what is now known as "The Seven Mountains" of society:

1. Religion
2. Family
3. Government
4. Business
5. Education
6. Arts/Entertainment
7. Media

*Invading the Enemy's Stronghold*s looks into many of these areas. While there is a dawning realization that we are to make disciples of and teach nations, we also have a need to develop instruction manuals and teachings on the "how-tos." How does one do that?

An important biblical tenet to understand in this process, taken from what Jesus called the greatest commandment: *"You shall love the Lord your God with all your heart, with all your soul, and with all your mind"* (Matthew 22:37 NKJV). We must know God's Word and be able to read the world in its light. A good reformer knows how to do this and does it adeptly. For instance, if you are called into government, you should know what the Bible says about this mountain.

The Bible is the Creator's handbook or manual. He has established certain laws and His world operates on them. It doesn't matter whether or not we believe they are true. Ignorance or disbelief in His laws does not negate our being subject to them. For instance, take the law of gravity. We may not like the law of gravity, and we may not believe it is real; however, it will go into effect if we jump off a tall building. We can say all the way down to the ground that we do not believe in it and should not be subject to it, but we will certainly hit the ground hard!

Most of the body of Christ is very good at understanding revival. There are many, many books written on the subject. (Of course, each generation needs its own revival voice.) In like manner, as we strive to find our place on the seven mountains, we need to understand we need to be informed reformers. This book could be called *Informed Reformation*.

I am excited to say more and more people know the church needs to leave the building and change society. For that to happen, we need to take the time to study and learn to love God with our whole mind as Matthew 22:37 tells us.

You will note that in order to know what to reform, you need to understand where our societies have taken a turn away from God. This helps us know what needs changing and where we need to start in each mountain. In order to do so, we need to understand God's Word.

> *Be diligent to present yourself approved to God, a worker who does not need to be ashamed, rightly dividing the word of truth* (2 Timothy 2:15 NKJV).

From there, we also get the importance of study or diligence in general. A reformer has to study.

I write about some of the great reformers in history in the following pages. My mentor, Peter Wagner, used to say, "If you don't know where you've been, you don't know where you are going!" You will learn about those who have gone before us and changed laws and brought justice. William Wilberforce was one of these. He spent his life to see slavery abolished in Great Britain in spite of poor health and living with pain. While he did not have good health, God gave him a convincing voice that convicted the heart of humankind. His voice rang out over and over in spite of the seemingly deaf ears and the seared consciences of Britain's lawmakers. Unfortunately, we had terrible slavery in the US as well.

As I studied the subject of reformation, something was kindled in my heart, soul, and mind—like a fire shut up in my bones. I want to see nations discipled and taught of the Lord, and I know that in order to do that I need to be a reformer. God calls us to not only convert individuals but to teach nations. As I mentioned, we need both revival and reformation to successfully invade the enemy's strongholds.

It is my heart's cry for you to become a reformer. I pray God's truth will spring to life inside of you as you read these pages. I also desire for the words I have labored to write for you to give you knowledge on knowing what to reform.

God is raising up a new generation of on-fire, passionate leaders in every sphere or mountain of society. Part of this leadership will include revivalists who are burning with a passion to see souls won and thousands saved on college campuses, in schools, and the streets of cities around the world. God is also going to raise up an army of nation-shaking reformers who

will march across the face of the earth with a new holiness movement.

No matter whether you are young or old, short or tall, in need of shedding a few pounds, red, yellow, brown, black, or white—God has called you to fulfill a destiny and purpose greater than yourself in your generation. It is time we stand together with the reformers of old and bring His light to the world.

Will you join me in learning how?

Let's begin!

NOTES

1. This was rectified in 2015 by the Spanish Parliament when they passed a law recognizing the descendants of the Jews expelled in 1492 as Spanish citizens. It was, however halted in 2019.

2. "The 10 most dangerous places for Christians," Open Doors, March 17, 2023, https:// www.opendoorsus.org/en-US/stories/top-10-most -dangerous-places-christians/; accessed March 6, 2023.

REFLECTIONS ON INFORMED REFORMERS

As I write this book to you today, you might be like many who are concerned about the state of the world around you, but you really don't know how to pray to change things. We can learn exactly how to pray in a way that will bring great change to our nations.

Sadly, many are ignorant of what satan has done and is doing to damage our families, as well as our nations. Scripture warns us that our archenemy will take advantage of us if we are ignorant.

> *Lest Satan should take advantage of us; for we are not ignorant of his devices* (2 Corinthians 2:11 NKJV).

How do we know how to strategically pray so not to be ignorant, but rather be an informed reformer? We need to learn how to spiritually map. Spiritual mapping is the study of a sector of society or a nation to see what they either have done in the past, or are presently doing, that is not according to Scripture.

In other words, it goes against the Creator's mandate given to us through His instruction, the Bible.

God's Word is given because He created the world to work in a certain way. When we follow His instructions, or commandments, everything works in a society. Why? Because all of creation multiplies and prospers when we obey His instructions. They are not capricious laws, given just because God wants to destroy our fun or individuality. They were made because the human body, interpersonal relations, and everything in the world thrives when God's laws are applied. In an opposite manner, when we break God's laws, individuals, families, churches, and every part of society breaks down.

So, spiritual mapping gives us an X-ray view of whatever part of society needs to be reformed. It shows us where to target our intercession, and then go out to change the spiritual climate of a nation.

No one can build a house without following blueprints. If we follow the blueprints, we will have the beautiful vision the architect designed. God designs nations certain ways with redemptive destinies and purpose; and in order to see the fulfillment of those plans, we must follow His commands. He is our Designer!

So how do we become an informed reformer? First, we must learn what is in the heavens to know what we are fighting. The book of Ephesians makes clear the importance of our job to intercede, as well as act, for this to transpire. In fact, the whole book is a magnificent statement of the authority we have through the name of Jesus. The very end of Ephesians is especially very important. Why? Because the last chapter is the summation of everything previously written.

Ephesians tells us to love one another, gives marriage and family counseling, and then ends with this scripture:

> *Finally, my brethren, be strong in the Lord and in the power of His might. Put on the whole armor of God, that you may be able to stand against the wiles of the devil. For we do not wrestle against flesh and blood, but against principalities, against powers, against the rulers of the darkness of this age, against spiritual hosts of wickedness in the heavenly places* (Ephesians 6:10-12 NKJV).

We use the title territorial spirits for these powers of darkness because they affect geographic regions.

So how do we begin to spiritually map a sector of society? We look into the sins of the people or industry involved in the mountain. This chapter has outlined the seven mountains of society that each have a strongman, or stronghold, attached to them. After we understand what the strongman is, we can then begin the process of informed intercession through the study to become informed reformers!

Why do we need to study the past? Critics might say we are just obsessed with history, and the past has nothing to do with our present intercession. This is ridiculous to me! The reason the territorial spirits are ruling is because they have been given legal right to establish a counterfeit kingdom! We must know where we have been in order to take away satan's legality and pull down the stronghold.

We begin with the study of the iniquities of the mountain of society for which we are called to intercede. With this knowledge, we know what to repent of when we are fulfilling our God-given command:

> *When I shut up heaven and there is no rain, or command the locusts to devour the land, or send pestilence among My people, if My people who are called by My name will humble themselves, and pray and seek My face, and turn from their wicked ways, then I will hear from heaven, and will forgive their sin and heal their land* (2 Chronicles 7:13-14 NKJV).

This Scripture passage refers to wicked ways. It is clear that something the people have been doing does not please God! When we add another significant Bible passage to the one in 2 Chronicles 7, we understand that it is not just present sin, but also past sin from which we must repent:

> *Now there was a famine in the days of David for three years, year after year; and David inquired of the Lord. And the Lord answered, "It is because of Saul and his bloodthirsty house, because he killed the Gibeonites." So the king called the Gibeonites and spoke to them. Now the Gibeonites were not of the children of Israel, but of the remnant of the Amorites; the children of Israel had sworn protection to them, but Saul had sought to kill them in his zeal for the children of Israel and Judah* (2 Samuel 21:1-2 NKJV).

In this passage, God is clearly saying that a drought has come on the land because of something Saul did that broke a promise the children of Israel made about 14 generations before Saul was king! God is the covenant-keeping God and He expects us to keep our covenants as well! In other words, the drought they were experiencing was because Saul broke a treaty or covenant that his ancestors made with the Gibeonites. Saul committed a sin that affected the whole nation. It was corporate in nature.

Let me give you an example:

The United States pretty much broke every treaty made to the Native Americans. Their land was stolen, many became diseased, their family life was disrupted, and many were killed or forcibly removed from their homeland, resulting what is known as the Trail of Tears.[1] To my knowledge, the pain was so great that very few Indians would accept what they called the "white man's gospel."

In the 1980s, many people began to understand the need to repent of this wickedness. People traveled to massacre sites and asked God to forgive. Meetings were held with the Native people, asking them for their forgiveness. Today, many Native Americans are rising up to take leadership to forgive in return, and the people are turning to God. In fact, redemptively, my friend, Chuck Pierce, along with Dr. Negiel Bigpond and other Native leaders, had a major gathering of the tribes here in the Dallas area. The strongman of racism against these great nations and peoples has been broken to a large degree. Of course, there is still much work to be done, but it is vastly different from forty years ago.

After you study and become aware of the sins done historically in a sector of society, you are ready to be an informed reformer who can legislate in the heavens the will of God to be done on earth as in Heaven.

How do we know the historic sins? Some of the big ones, such as I just referred to, involve racism against a particular people. For instance, for many years people of color were not allowed to act in movies. Incredulously, they would paint a White person's face black to "play" a Black actor in a film or production. This was done not only to portray Blacks, but Asians and Latinos as well. Racism! This practice ceased decades ago, but it is sad to say that racism is not dead and gone. In some areas of society, it can still be an active stronghold.

If you discover that racism is a major problem in the mountain of society that you either represent or are interceding for, you could pray a prayer like this:

> *Father God, I (we) come before You to repent for the sin of racism in Hollywood. I recognize it as sin. Please forgive the misrepresentation of the Black community, the ostracization, the closed doors, and the fact that we have caused harm and damage to the creative people whose destinies were meant to be in acting. Father, forgive and heal. Father, give restitution and open doors for people of all colors to fulfill their*

dreams and abilities. In Jesus's name, amen.

As you prepare yourself to be an informed reformer who invades the enemy's strongholds, you must make sure that there are no "holes in your armor," where satan has a legal right to attack you or cause backlash after your time of intercession.

I first learned about "holes in your armor" when I had an open vision of an intercessor boldly proclaiming they were putting on the armor of God—and saw that there were actually holes in the armor, which were entry points for satan to attack them. These holes were caused by unresolved wounds, lack of holiness, pride, and other such issues. They were actually unprotected!

Before going into spiritual battle, you must be battle ready! You simply do not declare against the strongman and think he will fall down. He wants to attack you as you attack him!

In preparing to do battle, it is important to surround yourself with intercessors who are praying as you go to war. I have heard many horror stories of people who did not properly prepare to do spiritual warfare.

The following are some steps to take to prepare:

1. Personal cleansing from unforgiveness, resentments, or woundedness.

2. As you prepare, make sure that you do not have iniquities in your own family line that would allow satan to attack. For instance, if you are dealing with the stronghold of mammon (finances), is there greed in your family line? Was your family involved in gambling, corruption, or the like?

3. Fasting is critical. Ask the Holy Spirit how long and what type of fast you need to do to prepare.

4. Prepare your spiritual mapping. Write a prayer guide to get others to agree with you.

5. Mobilize a prayer team to pray for you and those who are going on-site to pray with insight.

6. Don't forget to pray after your time of intercession so you will experience no backlash.

It is always safe to go after the strongman in these areas even if you don't have a huge prayer team:

1. Use "Identification Repentance," by repenting for the sin of the mountain of

society for which you are standing in the gap.

2. Read and declare God's Word concerning the sector of society.

3. Worship to bind the power of the strongman (Psalm 149).

By doing these things, you are actually legislating in the heavenlies in the court of Heaven that satan's power must come down. The following is a story of how this was done in a country:

Each year, violent storms would devastate this island nation. The Lord gave them the revelation to get the names of the storms for the next year from their weather bureau. They took the list and repented of any sins that gave satan the legal right to use the storms for destruction. Then, they began to legislate or decree before God, as the great Judge of the universe, that those storms had no right to devastate their nation. That next year, not one violent storm hit their coast.

Intercession like this is not a one-time thing and it is done. The leaders of the nations might openly worship idols, or commit sin against their own people or other nations during that year. We must continue to be a watchman on the wall of our nation from year to year.

People have asked me, "How many times do we need to repent?" My answer: until we see the change in our society. They also ask, "How much intercession does it take for the strongman to fall down?" My answer: until society manifests the changes that we are longing to see; abortion is abolished, God's natural design for gender and marriage is recognized, etc.

Ready, now let's read about people who stood in the gap to pray for their nations, for world missions, and parts of society!

NOTE

1. "The United States Government's Relationship with Native Americans," *National Geographic;* https:// education.nationalgeographic.org/resource/united -states-governments-relationship-native-americans/; accessed July 11, 2023.

PART TWO

PRAYER FOUNDATIONS FOR REFORMATION

CHAPTER 3

A HERITAGE OF PRAYER AND SERVICE

AS I STOOD on a windswept hill in Herrnhut, Germany, with a small group of friends, I could hardly believe where I was and wondered about those before us who might have stood praying in this same spot. For many years I had heard of the famous one-hundred-year prayer meeting of the Moravians, and now I stood in the village where it had all begun. The visit was unplanned in my agenda, but totally planned by God. It was another piece of the reformation puzzle He was putting together in my soul.

We had made a stopover in Prague, Czech Republic, as we traveled through five European nations on our way to Poland for another conference.

Our friend Lee Ann said to another friend JoAnna and me, "How would you like to go to Herrnhut on the way to Poland?" We only had to pray about one second before we shouted, "Yes, let's go!"

We were able to make tour arrangements with a descendant of one of the original praying Moravians, and off we went.

The village of Herrnhut was established in 1722 by Hussite refugees from Moravia—thus the name "Moravians"—fleeing persecution from the Counter-Reformation. Herrnhut means "The Lord's Watch." The land was owned as part of the estate of Count Nicholas Ludwig Zinzendorf, who was twenty-two years old at the time he granted them asylum.

Zinzendorf purchased the land from his grandmother, Baroness von Gersdorf, and he established the village of Berthelsdorf on part of it. Soon afterward he formed a group he called the "Band of Four Brothers" with three of his friends—Johann Andreas Rothe, pastor at Berthelsdorf; Melchior Schaffer, pastor at Gorlitz; and Friedrich von Watteville, a friend from boyhood. They met frequently for prayer and study and proceeded to stir up a small revival in the region. They printed and distributed large quantities of Bibles, books, tracts, and collections of hymns.

After the group's establishment, Zinzendorf moved to Herrnhut with his wife and children. The Moravians entered his life during this fertile time, but once the Moravians had escaped the external pressures of their previous home, strife and division tore at them from within. They had been driven fanatical by persecution and seemed to argue about everything. At one point they even turned on Zinzendorf and Rothe and denounced them as the Beast of the Apocalypse and his False Prophet.

Being a man of God, Zinzendorf stood steadily against the storm. Finally, on May 12, 1727, the community reached a turning point when Zinzendorf gave a three-hour address on the blessedness of Christian unity. The congregation fell into repentance, and a revival swept the village. The summer of 1727 was a golden one for the community whose hearts were again being knit together by the Holy Spirit, but God wasn't satisfied with a mere revival. In early August, Zinzendorf and fourteen other Moravian brethren spent a night in conversation and prayer. A short time later, on August 13, the community experienced "a day of the outpourings of the Holy Spirit upon the congregation; it was its Pentecost."[1] It was an experience that would change the world.

While in Herrnhut, I asked to see the cemetery called God's Acre where they brought the Moravian missionaries to their final rest after giving their lives in foreign nations. My friend James Goll had told me about it. As we stood on the hill just below the watchtower, I knew I was there to be marked by God like those who had gone before me. I knew that at some point during our visit I would be deeply changed.

Our friend Christian Winter, whose ancestors were among the Moravians who had prayed during those hundred years, walked us around and explained the area to us. (This is poignant for me now, as Christian has gone on to be with the Lord. He and his family were called to keep the twenty-four-hour watch of the Lord going in Herrnhut.) He explained that the men were buried on one side of the cemetery and the women on the other.

As we walked down the rows of markers, I noticed the names of countries on them—Suriname, Trinidad, and others. We walked past the crypt of Zinzendorf himself, and I began to tear up. The presence of the Lord was so strong. We knew this was holy ground.

Moving to another part of the cemetery, we again stopped and read the tombstones. "Who is buried here?" I asked Christian.

"The children of the missionaries who went to foreign fields," he answered. Then I noticed their markers had the names of countries also. Christian went on: "The people who went sent their children back to be educated at six years of age. Some who returned as a child never saw their parents again in this life. While a few became bitter, a number of them went back to the same countries where their parents had served." I was struck by this. I could feel the mark of God—a deep imprint of the purposes of God, the faithfulness of God, and the love of God—pressing into my soul.

One particular story that I'd heard was about a group of teenage boys who left on a boat as missionaries. Their parents were weeping, knowing they might never see their children again. The young men called back to their parents, "Mom and Dad, do not weep! We go for the Lamb and the cross!"

The cross and the Lamb. Yes, as I heard that story I knew that I had just received the strength I needed to continue with the message: Nations can be reformed through radical followers with revolutionary biblical principles to disciple nations. Those who had gone before me, and the story of their lives, reached out and marked my life that day forever.

Three strands wrapped around everything the Moravians did. James Goll writes about these in his book *The Lost Art of Intercession:*

1. They had relational unity, spiritual community, and sacrificial living.

2. The power of their persistent prayer produced a divine passion and zeal for missionary outreach to the lost. Many of them even sold themselves into slavery in places like Suriname in South America just so they could carry the light of the gospel into closed societies. The Moravians were the first missionaries to the slaves of St. Thomas in the Virgin Islands; they went to strange places called Lapland and Greenland and to many places in Africa.

3. The third strand was described by a motto that they lived by: "No one works unless someone prays." They took the form of a corporate commitment to sustained prayer and ministry to the Lord. This prayer went on unbroken for twenty-four hours a day, seven days a week, every day of each year for over one hundred years.[2]

Point three bears closer examination, as there was a marriage of intercessory prayer and work that we need to learn from in our generation. It seems to be reemerging today in the 24/7 prayer movement. This type of intercession is so important that I am going to spend a whole chapter dealing with its importance in reforming nations.

NOTES

1. A.K. Curtis, "A Golden Summer," www.zinzendorf .com/agolden.htm (accessed April 19, 2007). This article first appeared in *Glimpses* from the Christian History Institute.

2. James W. Goll, *The Lost Art of Intercession* (Shippensburg, PA: Destiny Image, 1997), 3-4.

REFLECTIONS ON A HERITAGE OF PRAYER AND SERVICE

History tells us that many people have gone before us who were devoted to changing nations and seeing nations evangelized. Many of them, like the Moravians you read about in this chapter, gave their very lives to intercede 24/7. We have wonderful examples of this today around the world. There is the International House of Prayer here in the United States in Kansas

City, and Pete Greig's 24/7 movement that began in Britain, to only name two of many.

I once asked the Lord, "Why do we need to pray 24 hours 7 days a week? Can't we just sleep at night and pray during the day only?" I felt the answer I was given was this, "Satan never sleeps and he has captured the night. I want My night back! I want it to be peaceful!"

In order to really see the reformation we need, we need 24/7 prayer to break open the heavens and see God's Kingdom will released. Our enemy has worked for many generations to establish his will, and now it is going to take a lot of intercession to reverse it!

While we all want Matthew 6:10 to take place and God's will released on earth, it is going to take informed reformers who will intercede and legislate into the heavens to bring about lasting change. This is so revival and reformation will lead to lasting transformation.

Let's pray:

> *Father God, raise up informed intercessors all over the face of the earth! Assign them to the mountains of society for revival to turn into reformation. Use me as one of those intercessors!*
> *In the name of Jesus.*
> *Amen.*

CHAPTER 4

THE UNITY OF TRUTH

ALTHOUGH THE STORIES of John Huss, John Wycliffe, Martin Luther, John and Charles Wesley, Count Zinzendorf, and the Moravians are divided by centuries in a world where communication was much more difficult than it is today, it is interesting that they hold so much in common.

For example, Luther spoke against many of the same things Huss did even when it is unlikely he was ever exposed to Huss's writings. Luther stood against indulgences and for a Bible translated into the common tongue so it could be understood by all.

One of Luther's major accomplishments was the translation of the Bible into German. That, coupled with the earlier invention of the Gutenberg printing

press, allowed copies of the Bible to be put into the hands of ordinary people. The Luther Bible contributed greatly to the convergence of the modern German language and is regarded as a landmark in German literature. The 1534 edition was also profoundly influential on William Tyndale's translation as well as the King James Bible.[1]

What literature did Huss, Luther, and Zinzendorf share in common that influenced them equally? More than anything else, it was the Holy Scriptures. These men came to unmovable faith in God and conviction of truth when they chose to look at the Bible as the basis of all things that pertain to life and godliness. It was the basis of the Reformation itself and is still the basis of individual, cultural, and national reformation today.

We need to realize that these men weren't great because of any special characteristics they had on their own. Luther was a man with feet of clay, and later in his life he became embittered at the Jews and wrote horrific things against them. While this is not to be excused, we can see that God also used Luther in great ways that are still touching us today. Why? Because when he lined up with God's Word, great and powerful transformation took place, and when he didn't, he fell into error like anyone else could. We need to get into the Word ourselves so that we can live according to it as much as the good examples of our past did.

As reformers, we must realize that we always stand upon the shoulders of those who have gone before us. Many of them paid a great price as groundbreakers in the truth so that we might have the liberty to live by the written Word today. This is why the generations must stay connected not only in relationship but also in knowledge. We need to know the path others have walked so we can build upon the foundation they have laid and not repeat their mistakes—especially when planning to invade enemy strongholds.

My mentor, Peter Wagner, paid a heavy price for being willing to release the new things that God is revealing to His people through the Scriptures. One day I was looking at a magazine and discovered that in the first half the writers were taking Peter to task for his writings on church growth, and in the second half they were criticizing his teachings about spiritual warfare. He once told me he just laughs at these things and checks to see if they have spelled his name right! While he was very interested in being biblically correct, he was not afraid of risk-taking or standing up for the unpopular things God showed him in the Word.

Peter Wagner went through a number of paradigm shifts during his many years of ordained ministry. One only has to read the seventy-plus books he wrote to

know that. He goes on in *Confronting the Powers* to relate about a time when he teamed with John Wimber during the power evangelism movement:

> In the 1980s John Wimber and I took a great deal of flak about power evangelism and our teachings on divine healing, miracles and casting out demons. Strong voices that still object to these on principle are now few and far between.[2]

While I have not gone through the firestorms anywhere near what Peter Wagner did, I can look back and remember the early-adopter stage for such topics as spiritual warfare, prophecy, and women in ministry, to name a few. Most of these movements are in the mid-to-late-adopter stage now. Of course, there are still some who are non-adopters and teach against those practices and doctrines.

Gilbert Bilezikian stresses an important point that all must learn to be a reformer when he says:

> Every generation of Christians needs to examine its beliefs and practices under the microscope of Scripture to identify and purge away those worldly accretions that easily beset us, and to protect jealously the freedom dearly acquired for us—both men and women—on the hill of Calvary.[3]

Today, just as in the times of Huss, Luther, and the Moravians, God is calling for believers of all generations to rise up, listen to the Holy Spirit together, and make adjustments to our religious structures without fear of persecution. There is too often a desire to resist something new God is doing for the sake of traditions that are not found anywhere in the Bible. Others want to keep their control and positions of power in a church body rather than letting God have His way. They choose to give in to religious spirits and legalism rather than let God touch lives and transform their communities. Such religious spirits are mean and sometimes deadly, but this should never stop us from following the Way, the Truth, and the Life.

This reminds me of a conversation I had one day with my preacher daddy, Albert S. Johnson. "Daddy," I quizzed. "What should I do if I find out the way we have believed on different issues isn't right?" My dad smiled that special kind of smile that made me feel like I was the most important person in the world and said, "Sweetheart, never be afraid to search for the truth. If you have it, you won't lose it." That was really good advice. It has given me the confidence to be an early adopter in several new moves of God without fear.

Fear cripples innovators. While we all may deal with it at times, as those called to be world changers we can't let it stop us. We have to be willing always to

speak the truth in love and stand up for the biblical convictions God has put into our hearts.

We follow in some big steps as we look back at the generations of reformers who have gone before us. Each of us will leave some kind of legacy to those who come after us as well. I want mine to be a good one, and I know you want yours to be as well.

NOTES

1. https://www.cambridge.org/bibles/bible-versions/ tyndale/new-testament/; accessed April 5, 2023.
2. C. Peter Wagner, *Confronting the Powers* (Ventura, CA: Regal Books, 1996), 32-33.
3. Gilbert Bilezikian, *Beyond Sex Roles* (Grand Rapids: Baker, 1985, 214, quoted in David Cannistraci, *The Gift of Apostle* (Ventura, CA: Regal Books, 1996), 86.

REFLECTIONS ON THE UNITY OF TRUTH

There are many reformers who have gone before us. While the level of intercession that backed them up is not always clear, as it is with the Moravians, we know that they could not have accomplished what they did without intercession. When God wants to move, He always gets His people praying!

I do believe that God is building a whole new-wine prayer network who will be aligned with the front-line reformers of today. There are many "hidden pockets" of people working in our present-day era who are faithfully working to bring both revival and reformation.

We each "stand upon the shoulders" of reformers like Martin Luther and William Wilberforce, as well as evangelists like John Wesley and George Whitefield. We must prepare ourselves to make a mark on society that others can follow.

I personally feel we all need to learn how to intercede over the sectors of society. Intercession may not be our main calling, but intercession ripens the harvest;

and we, at the least, need to be informed enough to raise up prayer warriors around our calling for revival and reformation.

Let's pray:

> *Father God, raise up many intercessors to do spiritual battle for the revival and reformation of nations. Show me my place on the wall, whether in prayer or as a forerunner, to bring biblical and long-lasting harvest and national discipleship.*
> *In Jesus's name.*
> *Amen.*

PART THREE

DISCIPLING NATIONS

CHAPTER 5

IMAGINE A WORLD

IMAGINE A WORLD where you turn on the television set and you don't have to screen what your children watch. Violent crime is unusual. The Internet doesn't need to be filtered for content. What about mega-cities where people ask, "What is the bad part of town?" and you reply, "My city doesn't have such a section. None of it is bad." Think about the possibility of grandparents walking their dog after dark in the inner city with no fear of being mugged. Imagine government social services and welfare offices closing down because those needs are being met by the local churches and faith-based nonprofits. Gang violence, homelessness, drug pushers, and drive-by shootings are all things of the past.

"Utopia?" you say.

"No," I would answer. "What I am describing is a nation discipled and taught of the Lord."

Did your heart leap within you as you read that first paragraph? Did a longing for it begin to grow? My heart yearns to see all of this come to pass in my city. Yet is this really possible, or do we have to wait until Christ's return? I am not saying that there will not be any more evil or sin in the world. However, just as there are areas of the world that are very safe, with little or no crime, I do believe that with the power of God, we can disciple our cities until this becomes the norm for us as well. Just look at how church-going communities differ from those where God is not known or valued.

How can we tip the balance in God's favor? Is it even possible? Let's consider some Scriptures together and see what you think for yourself. The concept of discipling nations doesn't begin with the last words of Christ on earth in the Great Commission. It all began in the garden.

The garden of Eden was a beautiful place, full of order, running according to God's design. God's law was universally obeyed. Adam and Eve, the first couple, were created in God's image with a purpose and given an earthly mandate:

> *Be fruitful and multiply; fill the earth and*
> *subdue it; have dominion over the fish of*
> *the sea, over the birds of the air, and over*
> *every living thing that moves on the earth*
> (Genesis 1:28 NKJV).

Do we still have that same purpose and mandate today as human beings created in the image of God? This dominion passage has never been rescinded, so our answer should be yes. It didn't change with the fall. It simply makes sense that God's original purpose for humanity on earth has never changed.

Being created in the image of God has a broad, sweeping scope that is governmental in nature. That government consists of a King and His appointed regents over His Kingdom on earth. Nelson's New King James Version Study Bible gives this insight into our being made in the image of God:

> In ancient times an emperor might command statues of himself to be placed in remote parts of his empire. These symbols would declare that these areas were under his power and reign. So God placed humankind as living symbols of Himself on earth to represent His reign. We are made to reflect His majesty on the earth, have dominion: Rule as God's regent.[1]

As I read those words I pondered to myself, *Why haven't we fulfilled that purpose?* Looking around the earth today one can certainly tell that we haven't even begun to fill, subdue, and have dominion over the earth in any positive way. Hebrews 2:5-9 acknowledges this. Instead we see poverty, violence, disease, homelessness, hunger, endless wars, and other major problems where the enemy has secured strongholds.

Our Genesis mandate to fill, subdue, and have dominion over the earth reminds us that God loves us, His children, but He also loves the world. He wants the world to be saved. He says so in John 3:16: *"For God so loved the world that He gave His only begotten Son."*

We tend to interpret this Scripture as referring only to our salvation from hell. While it does refer to that, salvation means a great deal more than escape from judgment. It also means that God loves His creation—the earth itself. Otherwise, why didn't John say, "For God so loved humankind that He gave His only begotten Son"?

We need to realize that Jesus's main emphasis was not the gospel of salvation but the gospel of the Kingdom of God. Jesus's first teaching was not "Repent so that you can be saved" or even "God loves you and has a wonderful plan for your life," but *"Repent for the kingdom of heaven is at hand"* (Matthew 4:17 NKJV). Jesus wasn't looking for converts to a new religion; He was inviting people into a new Kingdom, with a new government and a new King. He was inviting people to live Heaven on earth. (See Luke 4:18-19,21.)

In Jesus's own words, He said His Kingdom would address the poor, the mentally and emotionally ill, the physically sick, the blind, and those who sought justice. Jesus wasn't only creating the church; He was describing the new government of the Kingdom of Heaven.

Jesus wasn't looking to get people to change so much as He was looking to get kingdoms to change. He wanted to deliver God's people, and anyone else who would accept Him as Lord and Savior, out of the kingdom of darkness and into the Kingdom of light. He wanted to replace human justice—political, social, and religious—with God's justice. He wasn't looking to overthrow the power of Caesar but to usher all of the Roman Empire into the Kingdom of God.

God created the world—loves it still in all its creation—and has put us here on earth to be its stewards. We are His regents and ambassadors on earth. In other words, God so loved the world that He wanted not only us as individuals to be saved in every sense of the word but the systems of the world He created to be redeemed as well—to be bought back and brought back—to His initial plans for them. This includes the environment. We are still stewards of the earth as well as all living things in it.

NOTE

1. *Nelson's New King James Version Study Bible* (Nashville: Thomas Nelson, 1997), 5.

REFLECTIONS ON IMAGINE A WORLD

Being a reformer begins with dreaming. Intercessors need to stretch themselves to believe that God can do things far beyond what we think can change. We do that by reading God's world in the light of His Word, then using God's Word to cry out to Him to reform and return the nations we live in to His original design and purpose. God created everything and called it good. Our intercession binds the powers of darkness from making them bad. Reformers can make them good again.

Will you dream with me that God will use you to pray and act to change the world? Let's imagine a world without food deserts, where people can get enough to eat and where laws are just and corruption is rare. Can it happen? Of course! All things are possible for those who believe!

Let's pray:

Father, open my imagination and give me eyes to see where our societies are broken and we have strayed from Your divine intent for our nations. Reveal to me the prayers I need to pray, and then how to go and reform and restore society's sectors to biblical design so that Your will is done on earth as it is in Heaven.

In Jesus's name!

Amen.

CHAPTER 6

LIVING IN GOD'S KINGDOM ON EARTH

ONE OF THE new movements we are seeing develop in nation after nation today is in the marketplace or workplace. God is calling men and women to run their businesses according to biblical principles. Following this example, leaders in law, government, real estate, the sciences, and other institutions of society are also hearing God's call to return to His precepts in each of their fields.

One of the key concepts of the Reformation was *coram Deo*—all of life is lived "before the face of God." In other words, there was no separation between the sacred and the secular—you didn't do things Monday through Saturday that you needed to repent

of on Sunday. Instead, you lived all of life as though it were church all the time; only the means of worship changed day to day. On Sunday you might praise God with singing and listening to the Word, and on Thursday your praise may be in the way you performed your daily duties in the workplace and how you treated the people you interacted with.

My journey into being a reformer and discipler of nations actually began with my study on prayer. My first book, *Possessing the Gates of the Enemy,* is about intercession. I have been a student of prayers in the Bible throughout my ministry. At the time I wrote *Possessing,* I didn't fully understand how intercession and God's command that we have dominion on the earth tied together in this prayer. Note that the prayer is corporate in nature, not personal:

> *Our Father in heaven, hallowed be Your name. Your kingdom come. Your will be done on earth as it is in heaven. Give us this day our daily bread. And forgive us our debts, as we forgive our debtors. And do not lead us into temptation, but deliver us from the evil one. For Yours is the kingdom and the power and the glory forever. Amen* (Matthew 6:9-13 NKJV).

As I studied this powerful prayer, the thought came to me: *Do I really believe that I should pray for the will of God to be done on earth?* My next thought was: *What is God's will on earth now?*

I know there is a future Kingdom, but the Bible also speaks of the present Kingdom of God. What is possible here on earth today? What does the present Kingdom of God look like? Little did I realize that I was going through a radical, reformational shift in understanding my role on the earth as a believer in Christ.

After studying Matthew 6:9-13, I realized that this was a targeted intercessory prayer for one who is called not only to make disciples of individuals but of nations. If we are to pray for God's Kingdom to come and His will to be done, then it is imperative that we also learn how to do the will of God. Targeted intercession will unleash revival, awakening, and reformation.

As I read this prayer, I suddenly thought, *If part of this prayer is for the here and now—that we are to work to see God be Lord over not only our family affairs but our cities and nations—then the rest of the prayer must be understood in that same vein. It is not only for the individual; it is also a prayer of intercession for the nations.*

With that thought in mind, I began to study each part of the prayer.

"Our Father in heaven, hallowed be Your name." *Hallowed* according to Thayer's Bible Dictionary means "to render or declare holy, consecrate, or to separate from things profane and dedicate to God." We could paraphrase this by saying, "Father, holy is Your name." Because this is true, the inference biblically is "God, let Your name be holy and revered in every aspect of our Kingdom life. Holy be Your name in my neighborhood, my city, and my society."

"Give us this day our daily bread" has the broader meaning of petitioning God to give us a plan to feed the poor on a large scale and deal with systemic poverty around the world. It is holy and righteous to do these things, and God will help us to do them if we ask for His wisdom in how to do it.

Asking forgiveness for our own debts could include following God's economic plan to deliver people from poverty and the backbreaking bondage of always owing money to others. The borrower is, after all, servant to the lender (see Proverbs 22:7).

In fact, these premises are so broad in scope that I am going to take whole chapters and explore them as we delve into our role as believers on earth as it relates to justice, government, economics, education, and other Kingdom of Heaven issues addressed in this prayer.

If we are going to pray, "God's will be done," doesn't it make sense to look at what God's will is as expressed in the Bible? He made one part of His will clear in His last command to His disciples: "Go—disciple and teach nations" (see Matthew 28:19-20). We could rephrase the command to disciple nations in this manner: "Go and release the Jesus in you into every nation."

One could simply ask, "What would Jesus do and say about the problems we face in the world today?" However—if you would indulge me—let me give you a heavy-duty version of the same question: "How do we see the incarnated Savior manifested through us in society?"

Here are some synonyms for *incarnation:* integration, inclusion, incorporation, manifestation, and systemization. In other words, how do we see the Kingdom of God come into every aspect of society? What would it look like if God's wisdom and righteousness were incorporated into our laws, government, educational systems, as well as into our workplaces, homes, and everything we do?

If God's Word is systemic in how it applies to our needs for biblical justice—how we feed the poor and take care of single mothers, for example—letting it direct us in how we deal with each of these areas

releases the incarnation of that Word, Jesus Christ, into every situation.[1]

Social justice is not necessarily the same as biblical justice. Social justice may change as a society moves away from following God's Word. Biblical justice never changes in its principles in issues such as abortion and human trafficking and slavery.

Nations will be discipled when the incarnation of Christ is manifested at every level of society. To put it more simply, God wants His Word and presence felt in everything we think, plan, and do. Then everything is done "before the face of God" the way He has instructed us to do it. We are to be part of seeing His Kingdom manifest now while still understanding that there is a greater future Kingdom to come one day when Jesus returns.

NOTE

1. I wish to express my gratitude to Landa Cope, the first one whom I heard speak about this concept from Scripture of God giving His people a plan for the sectors of society. I honor and thank her for the initial ideas she taught in South Africa at the Congress on World Evangelism that set me on this path of discovery.

REFLECTIONS ON LIVING IN GOD'S KINGDOM ON EARTH

As believers, we are God's representatives, or ambassadors, on earth. As His representatives, we have authority to use the name of Jesus to speak His truth into each sector of society.

Many prophetic voices today are hearing that God is raising up modern-day Josephs and Daniels. They will be used by God to bring economic reformations to biblical economics. To even use the phrase "biblical economics" might sound foreign to us. Very few, if any, business schools offer a degree in biblical finance. Yet, the Bible gives us principles that impact the marketplace.

Maybe you are one of those Josephs or Daniels? Or perhaps you resonate with the word being given about a new generation of businesspeople who will see the transfer of wealth.

It is sobering to think that we, as God's people on earth, have not begun to grasp our job to disciple each sector of society. However, there is always a beginning! You can begin right now to be part of this new movement of informed reformers!

Let's pray:

> *Father, I want to be Your ambassador on earth. I want to bring all Your principles to manifestation into each sector of society. Raise up Josephs and Daniels who will be national advisors and financial planners. Use me to be part of seeing the great transfer of wealth that was prophesied in Proverbs 13:22.*
>
> *In Jesus's name.*
>
> *Amen.*

CHAPTER 7

THE GOSPEL OF THE KINGDOM

AFTER I HAD the revelation that the Kingdom of God was important in my time and that I had a role in seeing it implemented, I started studying my Bible with new excitement every day, trying to better understand God's Kingdom principles. One very important verse came alive for me:

> And this gospel of the kingdom will be preached in all the world as a witness to all the nations, and then the end will come (Matthew 24:14 NKJV).

"This gospel of the kingdom will be preached" echoed in my spirit as I read this. For my whole adult life, I had thought that we would preach the gospel of

salvation to all the world, and when everyone had heard, Jesus would return—but this is not what Scripture says. It says we should be preaching the good news of the Kingdom of Heaven. In other words, it is not so much about answered altar calls as it is about inducting people into a new government—God's Kingdom on earth. This gives me a much bigger responsibility for the world than I had previously understood.

Combining these two biblical passages—Matthew 24:14 with the Disciple's Prayer in Matthew 6:9-13—challenges us toward whole new levels as believers. And when you add Matthew 28:18-20—the Great Commission that commands us to disciple nations—into the mix, you can't help but experience an incredible paradigm shift. For me, it completely redefined how I saw my role as a believer on earth. We are not only to create converts, we are to manifest God's will on earth "as it is in heaven."

This led me to a new series of questions: "If this is true, then how do we preach the gospel of the Kingdom? What does it really mean to disciple or teach the nations of the earth? If we are called to disciple the world—and to love it as God loves it—how do we do that on a practical level?"

In the past I believed that when the gospel of salvation was preached in my city, it would change the fabric of society as well. I believed there is a correlation between the number of believers in a city and the godliness of government and culture in that city. For example, in a city with a large number of believers, poverty and corruption should be the exception, not the rule.

But as God was teaching me this, I began to wonder about my own city. I live in the Dallas/Fort Worth metroplex area of Texas. I know for a fact that Dallas/Fort Worth has a reputation as a densely Christian city. So does Colorado Springs, where our ministry was located before we moved back to our home area in Dallas. However, both areas have poor sections, and their city governments struggle with the same moral issues as most other US cities of their size. Though largely Christian, these areas are still not discipled and taught of the Lord.

Why is this? What's wrong?

It would seem that the number of Christians who live in an area should change the spiritual climate of that area, but I didn't have to look far before I saw that simply wasn't the case. Why is that? I think the answer lies in two main areas: 1) perhaps we as believers have not seen Kingdom living and building as our role; or 2) if we have, we don't know how to practically use biblical principles to change our cities into places where the will of God flows freely.

CREATING HOLY CITIES IN HOLY NATIONS

Imagine again for a moment what a place would look like where God's will freely reigned. A place where spiritual darkness is so weakened or defeated by the presence of light in the children of God that answers to prayer are unhindered, and God's blessings are available like fruit on trees that only needs to be harvested and distributed. A place where the body of Christ is alive and vibrant and healing flows to all that the body touches physically, emotionally, mentally, and spiritually. Certainly all would still have a right to freedom of religion, but people would know of Christians in every square foot of the city and respect them for their wisdom, conscientiousness, and loving-kindness toward others.

But this isn't happening because we as Christians are more influenced by our culture than we are by our Bibles. In the United States, we have accepted, for example, the separation of church and state as a good thing because of the corrupt church-run states of the past. However, the most horrific crimes of all time have not been perpetrated by church-run states. Even now in the US we are allowing atheists to have the loudest voice in dictating how we express religion in public places. Though we live in a democracy, we are allowing a minority to control the majority. Many Christians have dismissed being politically involved, and our nation has suffered for it. We look to human wisdom instead of God's for answers, and we are reaping a harvest of godlessness.

What we need is a radical shift in our worldview. We need to again see it as our responsibility to disciple nations and be radical reformers in our own nation. A key biblical building block in this process of shifting from a secular culture to a Kingdom-of-Heaven paradigm is found in both the New and the Old Testaments:

> *You are a chosen people, a royal priesthood, a holy nation, God's special possession, that you may declare the praises of him who called you out of darkness into his wonderful light. Once you were not a people, but now you are the people of God.... Dear friends, I urge you, as foreigners and exiles.... Live such good lives among the pagans that, though they accuse you of doing wrong, they may see your good deeds and glorify God on the day he visits us* (1 Peter 2:9-12 NIV).
>
> *Now therefore, if you will indeed obey My voice and keep My covenant, then you shall*

be a special treasure to Me above all people;
for all the earth is Mine. And you shall
be to Me a kingdom of priests and a holy
nation... (Exodus 19:5-6 NKJV).

Who was this last passage written to? A bunch of former slaves. Not only had they been slaves, but their parents and parents' parents also had been slaves. The people of God had been slaves for four hundred years. Did they know how to make laws, govern themselves, or even think for themselves? Of course not. They were slaves. Every day of their lives their actions were decided by others. Yet God didn't call them to a new religion—He called them to become a new nation and establish a new Kingdom.

This is why God began to give them the "how-tos" concerning becoming a Holy Nation after the Exodus. This included the structure for government, legislative systems, judicial systems, as well as educational and economic systems. For instance, Deuteronomy 1:9-15 and Exodus 18 talk about a representative government where leaders were chosen from each tribe and set over groups of one thousand, one hundred, fifty, and ten. If the people of God followed the structure He gave them, it would result in transforming a nation of slaves into one of the wealthiest and most prosperous peoples on earth.

What does this mean for us today? Romans 11:16-24 tells us that we are the children of Abraham, grafted into the vine, with the full benefit package given to the children of Abraham. All of these points revolve around the fact that God called the sons of Abraham to be a Holy Nation—a call we as Christians have as the children of Abraham as well. How do we, in a practical way, function as a Holy Nation across the face of the earth today? I will pose some exciting possibilities in answer to that question in the pages and chapters to follow.

Becoming a Holy Nation may seem like a big stretch for us given the fact that some of us have trouble even working together as a church and that religious government has such a bad track record. I mean, we are still trying to get over the damage done during the Crusades! After all of this you might ask, "How could we possibly work together as a Holy Nation to see His Kingdom come and His will be done?"

I know that some are reeling as you are reading this and might be thinking, *Cindy, are you advocating an authoritarian takeover by Christians?*

No, of course not. I am not saying that we should use physical force to disciple nations, but rather we should establish ourselves through a spiritual revolution. Righteous reformers must take seriously their role in discipling nations from a Holy Nation worldview.

The biblical mandate to disciple nations is one that many leaders are working to understand. It is a concept that can help them manifest God's Kingdom in their nations. In fact, God has given the desire to transform nations to many in leadership around the world—and, believe it or not, it is making a difference.

REFLECTIONS ON THE GOSPEL OF THE KINGDOM

I am excited to see that many people around the world are preaching about the Kingdom of God. This is important because we know we are part of the future Kingdom, but there is also a present Kingdom.

As a child, I always felt that Jesus would come back when everyone had the opportunity to be saved. While this is critical and eternal, I now know that our Kingdom mandate is much more expansive than I once understood.

I believe we should regularly pray and decree: Let Your Kingdom come and Your will be done on earth as it is in heaven. Intercession should be Kingdom-minded. We can literally pray the will of God into the earth.

I realize this expanded job description can be daunting. That is because we have so much catch-up to do from generations who have not understood their complete job description. The good thing to know is that we will also see supernatural acceleration far beyond and greater than we could imagine or dream. When we engage God's Word into the earth, all kinds of angels begin to war for His will to be done. The powers of darkness, as we know, are simply no match for the supernatural power of God!

This is even more exciting when we factor in that millions of believers are awakening to the truth that we can see the gospel of the Kingdom come into fruition through our prayer and actions. The Bible proclaims that one will put a thousand to flight, and two will put ten thousand. Imagine the factor that takes place when millions are warring against the enemy's plans in our nations! It's almost unfathomable!

Let's pray:

Father God, I am excited to partner with You in seeing Your will done on earth. I now know I am made for so much more than I ever realized or dreamed!
In Jesus's name.
Amen.

CHAPTER 8

RESTORATION OF ALL

THE BIBLE IS our Manufacturer's handbook. In it, God gives specific instructions on how the world best operates. It belongs to Him as Creator. He knows how to make it work.

To say to the Creator, "I can run this world the way I want to, do what I want with it, enact laws in the society about morality the way I want, and do anything that I want with my private life as long as I don't hurt anyone else," is totally ridiculous! Many things done "in private" hurt others. The "secret sins" of pornography and adultery are tearing our families apart; and the sins that societies allow within their midst build up until the very ground cries out to God just as Abel's blood did after Cain murdered him.

That thinking could be likened to a person who has never owned a cell phone and doesn't read the instruction manual on how to use it. Instead, the person decides, "I don't need to turn the phone on the way the manual says; I want to start it the way I want to!" It simply won't work that way! We have to do what the instruction book says in order to make it work.

In the same way, we can't enact laws that condone immorality simply because it is done in "private," or any other action that breaks God's rules. When you break God's law, creation breaks down—and societies do too.

During the years that Mike and I have had the ministry Generals International (originally founded as Generals of Intercession), we have worked in many nations that are in the process of transformation. Some of the brightest lights on earth have lost their place of transformation.

Several years ago Mike and I had the privilege of sitting in a government office while an official humbly repented for breaking treaties with the Native Americans. The Native American leaders had brought a volume listing all the treaties made with various tribes, and every one had been broken. The government leader held the thick book in his hands and with deep emotion prayed, "Father, I ask You to forgive the government that I represent for our sin against the host people of the land, the Native American people. I am so sorry for our sin." He then looked at the Native leaders and asked for their forgiveness as well.

This is a beautiful picture that is part of the fulfillment of Revelation 22:2:

> *In the middle of its street, and on either side of the river, was the tree of life, which bore twelve fruits, each tree yielding its fruit every month. The leaves of the tree were for the healing of the nations.*

As we become healed nations or peoples in our earthly identities, it will become increasingly easy for us to function as one. Just as it was for those at Herrnhut, unity is a key to our transformation and reformation today.

For the past twenty years, our ministry has been working to see this kind of healing happen in all the nations to which we have traveled. However, there is still quite a bit of work to be done in this area. Racism, prejudice, and dishonest dealings between nations remain in the world, and this kind of repentance and reconciliation will need to continue. We'll never be able to say we're completely finished with this process, because each generation will need to acknowledge its unique dirty history.

If each generation doesn't do this, it can convince itself that its ancestors were pure and not responsible for atrocities in the past, and that it was on the wronged side and therefore needs to take vengeance into its own hands. A false belief in a myth of purity is dangerous to anyone who happens to be outside their group. However, the major paradigm shift that I see in this new move of God is adding the dimension of reconciling all things to the list of reconciling all races.

The book of Acts tells us:

> *Repent therefore and be converted, that your sins may be blotted out, so that times of refreshing may come from the presence of the Lord, and that He may send Jesus Christ, who was preached to you before, whom heaven must receive until the times of restoration of all things...* (Acts 3:19-21 NKJV).

What does this passage mean by "all things"? My husband, Mike, teaches this "all things" restoration from Paul's letter to the Colossians:

> *For it pleased the Father that in Him all the fullness should dwell, and by Him to reconcile all things to Himself, by Him, whether things on earth or things in heaven, having*

made peace through the blood of His cross
(Colossians 1:19-20 NKJV).

Mike points out that the Scripture doesn't say "all people" but "all things." "All things" means "all things." "All things" means "all structures, all parts of society, all groups of people." In fact, we have the ministry of reconciliation on earth given to us as an assignment by God to reconcile all things (see 2 Corinthians 5:17-19).

What do you think has been the major deterrent to our transforming or discipling our nations? I have a theory that it has been our understanding of where we should expend our time and energy in this season before the Lord's return.

Remember that we were commanded by the Lord to "do business till I come" in the parable of the minas (see Luke 19:12-27). The King James Version says, *"Occupy till I come."* It may be that our focus has been so much on the Lord's return that we missed the "occupy" part of our instruction. Part of our occupying is evangelism—to bring people to Christ and nurture them until Christ is fully formed in them.

Another part is to fulfill the Genesis mandate to be fruitful, subdue, and have dominion over the earth (see Genesis 1:28). We are stewards of God's earth in every sense. Yet how do we "occupy" the business world, legal and legislative systems, government agencies and public services, educational institutions, and other sectors of society crucial to letting God's "goodwill toward men" reign in our nations? (See Luke 2:14.)

REFLECTIONS ON THE RESTORATION OF ALL

There is a prophetic promise given in Acts 3:19-21 that gives a bold proclamation. It says Jesus will be in Heaven until the restoration of all things. That is an absolutely mind-boggling statement! While I am sure the theologians have many differing thoughts on this Scripture in Acts 3, let me pose one to you: What if "all things" really means "all things" and could "all things" mean that our nations need to be discipled and taught of the Lord?

The very thought that nations can be healed is painted for us beautifully in the very last book of the Bible. It says that the tree of life is for the healing of the nations (see Revelation 22:2). Amazing! Nations can be healed.

If they can be healed, this means they also can be sick. God want to use us as informed reformers to make them well.

Let's pray:

> *Father God, as I look at my nation through the lens of Scripture, it looks pretty dire! However, your Word promises that nations can be healed. Would You give me the revelation of how I can be used to heal my nation? Show me my part and I will be obedient to do whatever it takes to see its restoration.*
>
> *In Jesus's name.*
>
> *Amen.*

PART FOUR

ATTACKING THE STRONGHOLDS— HEAVENLY LEGISLATION

CHAPTER 9

ATTACKING STRONGHOLDS

SATAN IS A strategist. Only a few years before that "Summer of Love" in 1967, Bible reading and prayer were officially removed from public schools. From then on, millions of children stopped hearing God's truths in school every day, acknowledging God as the Creator and Ruler of the universe. It is not hard to see a connection between these events.

As we look at the educational system here in America—where the influencers of the nations send their children to be prepared for life—we should consider this warning from Romans:

> *For the wrath of God is revealed from heaven against all ungodliness and unrighteousness of men, who suppress the truth*

in unrighteousness, because what may be known of God is manifest in them, for God has shown it to them. ...men, leaving the natural use of the woman, burned in their lust for one another, men with men committing what is shameful, and receiving in themselves the penalty of their error which was due. And even as they did not like to retain God in their knowledge, God gave them over to a debased mind, to do those things which are not fitting; being filled with all unrighteousness, sexual immorality, wickedness... (Romans 1:18-19,27-29 NKJV).

So what are we to do? Many in America have taken the avenue of homeschooling their children or sending them to private Christian schools. Those are good and viable choices that are even now being threatened in the United States. However, what about all the other children in our nation? What is our moral responsibility toward them? How do we, indeed, reverse what has happened in our schools? There are parents in other nations who have been arrested for homeschooling their children. Why? Because the government believes that only it can adequately teach values to their children—among other things.

And what about nations that don't have private Christian education? What about the poor who cannot afford to send their children to private schools or buy curriculum for homeschooling? Do we simply abandon these kids to social Darwinism and humanism?

First of all, we need a prayer strategy. There is a discussion about "Legislating in the Heavens" in the next chapter and in the upcoming Part Five with details how to begin to break the strongholds that have developed through false teaching. We must take seriously our role in invading the enemy's bastions.

Second, we need to be informed. What are your children being taught? Look at their textbooks and listen in on their classes as an observer. Take a tour of the school's library.

Third, find out what the universities and colleges in your area are teaching. If you find something shocking in the courses, let others know and make a formal complaint to the leadership. Find out who funds the schools and write to them. Protest to your government leaders if you find something offensive.

Fourth, get involved in the system. By this I mean, encourage Sunday school students to become public schoolteachers. Children should be raised with the idea of becoming missionaries to the school systems. Teachers, God will anoint you to be change agents in

children's lives around the world. You are called as holy revolutionaries to your school.

Fifth, churches need to get involved with the public schools. Find out when school board elections are taking place and unite with the pastors and other leaders in your area to elect godly people to have control of what goes on in the school district.

I encourage pastors to understand that you have a critical role to play in the worldview of your people. The pastors of churches in every nation have always, historically, been a voice for righteousness. Appoint a liaison from your church to keep you informed about the schools in your area. Make an appointment with the mayor or other top government official in your city and talk with your congregation about what you have learned.

There is a great underground movement taking place of Christian parents who are informed about the conditions of the public schools. Private Christian schools and the homeschooling movement around the world are keys to changing the nations, but we must also infuse the public schools with righteousness to transform nations.

If you are currently a schoolteacher, find other teachers willing to pray together. God wants to reverse the Humanist Manifesto and its tentacles over the face of the earth. Accept the call of God as a reformer in the school system. Form prayer groups in your schools.

Pastors, adopt the teachers of your area in intercession. At the same time, all Christians must pray for revival to break out across the nations of the earth. We must teach our children both in church and in the home that they are called of God to reform their nations according to God's societal rule book—the Bible. After that, we will begin to see righteousness rise up in our lands, and we will fulfill the biblical mandate to teach nations to observe all things that He has commanded us.

REFLECTIONS ON ATTACKING STRONGHOLDS

As we look at the schools of our nations, it doesn't take the gift of discernment to realize our generations are under attack! Anti-biblical ideologies have been taught for years in our schools. There is a stronghold over the education sector, or mountain, that has been working its way into the thought lives of our children while we paid for it with our tax money.

This stronghold is called humanism.

How do we develop a prayer life that counteracts humanism? First of all, we need to be informed as to what it is and what it does. The time when we could just sit back and blissfully send our children off to school with lunch money or a sandwich is over.

To pray correctly, we need to be informed intercessors. There are real spirits fighting against our teachers, administrators, and schoolchildren. We need to develop a strategy to both pray and act—prayer activism.

How do we go about being informed? I suggest you either join a prayer group for your schools, or form one yourself. Also, if you are student, form a prayer club. Be pro-active! I have found that God is usually calling us to be an initiator of prayer when we say things like, "Why doesn't somebody do something about this problem?!" When a situation really bothers you, it might be that God is trying to stir you to action!

If you can't find someone to pray with you, make that a point of your prayers! Ask God to give you a prayer partner! The person doesn't necessarily have to be a parent of a student in school, all they need is a heart to pray. Another suggestion is for churches to adopt the schools in their locality.

And if you are homeschooling your children, pray for the public schools. While protecting our families from humanism at home by teaching a biblical worldview, we can't sit idly by and allow public-schoolchildren to experience only a secular worldview. Consider that all of the children in the United States, without exception, were once taught their lessons from Scripture. The most important lessons in life were based on the ABCs; they would have learned:

A: All have sinned and fallen short of the glory of God (Romans 3:23).

B: Believe on the Lord Jesus Christ and you will be saved (Acts 16:31).

C: Confess with your mouth, the Lord Jesus Christ (Romans 10:9).

The founders of the United States considered the Bible so important to the education of our children that they ordered Bibles to be distributed to schools. How far we have fallen! This has all happened because we Christians have not stewarded and discipled our school systems. We have allowed "activists" to control the school boards and they are injecting LGBTQ ideology into our schools without giving parents an

opportunity to even voice an opinion about what the children are being taught. Five-year-olds are not emotionally or mentally mature enough to be exposed to these issues. Indoctrination! An informed intercessor knows what curriculum is being taught in the schools.

Let's talk about university-level education. Many of us are shocked at the concepts, theories, and so-called truths taught in colleges and universities today. Some Christians students become disillusioned about their faith, and some even fall away from following the Lord. Many of those who stand for their faith are battered by liberal professors—and some have been refused entry to Ivy League schools after being identified as being "Christian." To an extent, we are living a form of captivity—a jail of our making by virtue of either complacency or ignorance in our reluctance to make our voices heard about the godly precepts that made our nation a once-great model for the world. The good news is that God is a prayer-hearing God! (I think I'm starting to preach a bit here!)

A group of students at Arizona State University in Tempe, Arizona, actually "spiritually mapped," or studied, the founding of various aspects of their campus. What they discovered was egregious! However, they made a "road map" of intercessory prayer to study how to invade the darkness and bring God's light to the university.

We must attack the darkness in our schools. Get active; believe that with God we can restore our school systems to their original godly intent to teach children biblical values and skills to advance God's Kingdom and enhance our communities and nation.

Let's pray:

> *Father God, I realize that there are strongholds that have been built up for many generations. Lord, allow me to invade the enemy's camp with courage and resolution through spiritual warfare.*
>
> *In Jesus's name.*
>
> *Amen.*

CHAPTER 10

LEGISLATING IN THE HEAVENS

THE AIR IN the room was electric. A group of dedicated leaders had come together in Washington, DC, to "shift the nation." The Lord had shown us that we were to convene what amounted to a prayer court to intercede for the United States.

Just that day, Mike and I had taken a side trip to tour the Supreme Court building. As we walked up to the facility, we noted a little sign that read: The court is in session. Please enter by the side door.

The fact that the court was in session that day was significant because we were about to pray some radical prayers that evening, which we believed would begin to turn the tide against unrighteousness in our nation. The date was June 22, 2006.

It is interesting how the Holy Spirit is in control of our lives, ordering our footsteps, even when we are not aware He is doing so. I often wonder if we could peel back the veil between the visible and invisible worlds, would we see the Lord's angels orchestrating our movements? Personally, I believe we would. That thought is very, very comforting to me.

While taking a preliminary tour of that particular building the day before, I had stopped in the gift shop and picked up a gavel and block engraved with the words, The Supreme Court of America. At the time I thought, *What a great souvenir!* But the next day I knew that it was more than a souvenir. God wanted us to use it as a symbol of His judicial authority over the nations. We were to convene the court of heaven and legislate His will in the earth—and I would call that court to order using this gavel.

That night, as the meetings began, I felt we were to appeal to God as the great Judge of the universe concerning the unrighteous laws of our nation. I took the gavel and pounded it on the block, grabbing the attention of everyone in the room. Then I announced the vision that God had shown me: The Captain of the Lord of Hosts was waiting to come into the city with angels riding on chariots of fire. They were encircling the area and making way for His righteousness. (By the way, there was a war in the natural as well—the air conditioner was broken, and our skin glistened as we went into prayer and worship.)

During the time of worship, I stepped to the platform and began to prophesy: "I am going to wash Washington, says the Lord!" This "shifting of the nation" and our prayer assignments were set in motion through the prophetic words released that first night of the conference. The speakers were Dutch Sheets and Chuck Pierce. Dutch stood and shared that a prophet, Sam Brassfield, not knowing that Dutch was on a flight to Washington, DC, had called his home to find him. He later connected with Dutch and gave him the word: "God says, I am going to wash Washington." Dutch went on to explain that he thought it was just a funny saying, until I got up and stated the same thing! Chuck Pierce, as he often does, tag-teamed as we flowed together in the Spirit and prophesied that the city was going to flood.

We asked Thomas, a youth leader who worked with Lou Engle and The Call movement, to pray and ask God to send His chariots of fire into the city to do war over unrighteous laws, such as those legalizing abortion. Thomas was himself almost a statistic on the list of aborted babies and prayed with great authority.

That night after the meeting, the skies over the Capitol looked like the bombing of Baghdad. Lightning and thunder rocked the skies, and rain began to fall. Over the weekend the rain increased, and

the skies reflected what was going on in the spiritual, invisible realm, with angelic hosts fighting the powers of darkness over the city. There was a war going on in the heavenlies!

The news services on Monday, June 26, 2006, reported in the natural what the prophets had prophesied at our Shift the Nation conference. There was so much rain, one part of the city was flooded and a five-foot deep mudslide buried the Capital Beltway for one mile. This, we felt, was a sign that corruption was going to be exposed in DC, and an Isaiah 35 "highway of holiness" movement would take place in the political system.

That is not all. Constitution Avenue flooded, as did the Justice Department and the Internal Revenue Department. Fish were found flopping in the streets from the deluge!

Part of our intercession was about the original design of the city by a Freemason named Pierre Charles L'Enfant. The metro-rail subway system at the L'Enfant stop was closed due to water on the electrical lines.

One final and significant sign happened in the days following our prayers. During these prayer times, I kept declaring that I saw the hand of God rocking a large tree back and forth and that it would be pulled up by its roots. A large elm tree—one of a pair located on the lawn of the White House—was uprooted during the storm and had to be replaced. (These two trees flank the White House in the picture on back of the twenty-dollar bill.) We saw this as another indication that hidden corruption would be exposed. (A second tree has since been planted.)

REFLECTIONS ON LEGISLATING IN THE HEAVENS

When God created the earth, He not only made things we can see with our natural eyes, but He also created an invisible realm. It is important to understand that we were put on the earth to steward both the seen and unseen. We can understand the unseen realm as being the angelic and demonic, including various levels of such beings. How do we know what has been established illegally over various mountains of society? We look for what manifests in our culture.

For since the creation of the world His invisible attributes are clearly seen, being understood by the things that are made, even His eternal power and Godhead, so that they are without excuse (Romans 1:20 NKJV).

If we see the invisible things of God through the things He has made, the counterfeit of that are the invisible attributes of the ungodly principalities and powers over our nations revealed through their societal manifestations. What are some of these?

THE MUSIC CULTURE

What does society predominately value? Cultural music such as hip-hop and rap are not necessarily evil, but when the lyrics are primarily about sex, killing, and other such evils, then we know the powers of darkness have a legal stronghold to affect the nation. These profanity-filled songs sell by the billions. Who buys this music? Our children, which reflects the soul of the nation. We have lost too much of our culture. Only a massive revival and reformation can change this situation. The salvation of the artists who put out these kinds of lyrics is at stake. We must pray for them.

THE ARTS

What kind of artwork is produced and paid for by our cities and nations? Much of the art in the early days of many nations were Freemasonic in nature. When studying Freemasonry, you can tell that at the highest levels they worship the "Great Architect," not Jesus. Some of the masons use the name of Jesus, but those who understand know that the whole belief system behind this secret society is not biblical at all. This was recognized by the great revivalist, Charles Finney, who wrote a book against Freemasonry titled, *The Character, Claims and Practical Workings of Freemasonry*. People would openly renounce Freemasonry in his revival meetings.

PUBLIC CELEBRATIONS

What do people today openly celebrate other than national holidays? Sad to say, throughout the nations, homosexuality is openly celebrated. This is a very serious sin. While we do not support and vehemently oppose hate crimes against anyone in homosexuality, Romans 1 gives strong language that we are not allowed to participate in such behavior.

The list of ungodly societal manifestations can go on, but I think you understand my point. When we study our cities, we then can go to the great Judge of the universe to plead our legal biblical case in the court of Heaven that these behaviors should not be allowed to continue. I have been told many times that we cannot legislate morality, and I declare, "Not true!" We do it every day! We cannot murder or steal without consequence. However, even the boundaries of how much stealing should be allowed has changed in some states in the US. Some police are not permitted to arrest criminals for "petty crimes" such as stealing under a $1,000 worth of goods.

I am not advocating the removal of civil rights, but I believe when the margins have moved in our schools to where a parent has no say in the gender transitional surgery of their child, what is deemed civil rights has turned upside down.

How do you legislate in the heavens?

1. Determine what is unlawful in God's eyes.
2. Find Scripture to back up your case.
3. Come before the court of Heaven to legislate your case before the great Judge of the universe.
4. Decree and legislate that what is unlawful in Heaven is unlawful on earth.
5. Then say out loud, "Let Your will be done on earth as it is in Heaven!" Amen.

Let's pray:

Father God, open my spiritual eyes and ears to understand the authority I have in the name of Jesus. Use me to legislate in the heavens to see that Your judicial will is done on earth as it is in Heaven.

In Jesus's name.

Amen.

PART FIVE

HEAVENLY LEGISLATION THROUGH INTERCESSORY PRAYER

CHAPTER 11

STEWARD THE HOUSE

OUR ROLE IN seeing God's will done on earth began in the garden. Going back to the premise that we are to "steward the house"—the earth—we need to understand our roles as intercessors in Genesis mandate to *"Be fruitful and multiply; fill the earth and subdue it; have dominion"* (Genesis 1:28 NKJV). Our stewardship not only includes things in the seen realm but also things in the unseen realm. In other words, we must take authority over the unseen (spiritual) realm that affects the seen (natural) realm. We have a saying here in the US: "There is more to this than meets the eye," or, there is more happening than we can see.

An important spiritual axiom in this regard: Stewardship of God's creation requires strategic, targeted intercession in order to see God's will done on earth as it is in Heaven. This intercession must break down the demonic powers behind the ideological structures that influence people's thinking in areas such as humanism, poverty, and abortion.

There were things set in motion in the fall of Adam and Eve that need to be reversed through prayer. In order to steward all of creation, we must not only deal with what we see in the natural realm but also address the supernatural structures—called strongholds—that must be broken in the heavenlies to see God's will done on earth. Ephesians 6:12 (AMPC) makes this clear:

> For we are not wrestling with flesh and blood [contending only with physical opponents], but against the despotisms, against the powers, against [the master spirits who are] the world rulers of this present darkness, against the spirit forces of wickedness in the heavenly (supernatural) sphere.

I call this kind of intercessory prayer legislating in the heavens. Let me explain: When the Congress of the United States meets—or Parliament in the United Kingdom, Australia, etc.—they legislate, or make laws. In legislating in the heavens, we decree through intercessory prayer that God's laws will be the laws of our nations. We also declare His will be manifested in every area of life and society.

Daniel 7:26-27 (NKJV) gives us a picture of this court of Heaven:

> *But the court shall be seated, and they shall take away his dominion, to consume and destroy it forever. Then the kingdom and dominion, and the greatness of the kingdoms under the whole heaven, shall be given to the people, the saints of the Most High. His kingdom is an everlasting kingdom, and all dominions shall serve and obey Him.*

As intercessors of the Lamb, we serve as "assistant advocates" of the Kingdom, charged with defending the King's people and prosecuting the King's enemies in the spirit realm (the adversary and his rebellious followers). Each time we come before the "bench" of the Judge of All, our Chief Advocate comes alongside and takes us by the arm to formally present us before the Judge and enumerate the legal credentials that He has delegated to us. We "practice before the bar" as lawyers sent from His high office—the Chief Intercessor and Chief Advocate of the redeemed.[1]

Our training as intercessors must include the presenting of a legal, biblical case before the throne of

God. As we do this, the Holy Spirit begins to intervene in the affairs of people, laws, and nations to bring about the changes needed to establish His righteousness. In addition, the blessings of God will begin to pour out from Heaven upon the nations of the earth because of that righteousness. This is why this kind of reformation intercession is so important. If we are to be reformers, we must reform the structures of the heavens as well as the earth because both are part of God's creation! There are dominions, or heavenly places, that hold whole sectors of society under their wicked sway and must be defeated through intercessory prayer.

A synonym for *dominion* is *kingdom*. Another way to think about our call as intercessors would be to paraphrase Matthew 6:10 this way: "Let Your dominion come on earth, as it is in heaven."

Some nations are known as dominions, such as the Dominion of Canada. One of the Scriptures the founders chose as a cornerstone for our nation is Psalm 72:8 (NKJV):

> *He shall have dominion also from sea to sea, and from the River to the ends of the earth.*

I am aware that the term *dominion* has been given a bad name by those who have theologically abused it.

However, I feel strongly that we cannot let this good biblical term be preempted because of wrong usage.

The Bible gives us sound doctrinal reason to take dominion over the powers of darkness and establish God's will—or dominion. We do this by prevailing against the powers of darkness and by reminding God of His laws and promises in Scripture. It is not that He forgot them, but He wants to see our faith in action as His legal representatives on earth. He has given us authority here on earth and will not usurp that authority; but if we come to Him and ask that His promises be fulfilled and His laws enforced, then He will do just as He has written. There are several other passages that point to this doctrine of reformation intercession, such as Colossians 1:16 (NKJV):

> *For by Him all things were created that are in heaven and that are on earth, visible and invisible, whether thrones or dominions or principalities or powers. All things were created through Him and for Him.*

Since God created His order in Heaven and earth, both in the visible and invisible realms, it stands to reason that when satan began to set up his demonic, invisible structures he would counterfeit God's plan. Ephesians 1:20-23 (NKJV) gives us another biblical snapshot of heaven's authority over satan's counterfeit systems:

> *Which He worked in Christ when He raised Him from the dead and seated Him at His right hand in the heavenly places, far above all principality and power and might and dominion, and every name that is named, not only in this age but also in that which is to come. And He put all things under His feet, and gave Him to be head over all things to the church, which is His body, the fullness of Him who fills all in all.*

Simply put, we must establish God's Kingdom according to His divine rule in each sector of society by dethroning the powers of darkness that hold the nations in their grip—successfully invading the enemy's strongholds.

NOTE

1. Notes received by email from David Thompson, vice president of Transform Our World, March 1, 2021.

REFLECTIONS ON STEWARD THE HOUSE

Building on the theme of legislating in the heavens and convening the courts of Heaven is important. We learned in this chapter how to steward God's earth. Stewarding God's earth in our generation, of course, must connect with the Scripture I ended with in the previous reflections devotional, "Let Your will be done on earth as it is in heaven." We could take this as a reference to go back to our original, created design from the garden when we were commanded to take dominion over creation.

We might understand that when God created the earth, it was intended to be a colony of Heaven. There was no sin and no curse working in Heaven, and we were to care for God's creation here.

I spent the beginning part of my life believing that I should not try to improve the earth, as it was just going to eventually be burned up anyway. It was the world, and I was getting out of it as fast as possible to enter my eternal reward. Even if the Christian world in general did not fully believe what I did, our actions reveal our hearts. Nations belong to God! He loves all of His creation. John 3:16 (NKJV) tells us:

> *For God so loved that world that He gave His only begotten Son, that whoever believes in Him should not perish but have everlasting life.*

Of course, everlasting life means salvation, which is primary! We need to get people saved. But He also loves the nations He created. He wants us to love the nation where we live too! This is why we must pray and discern the will of God for our country.

I have been sharing about informed intercession, or spiritual mapping. Spiritual mapping is simply a term that allows us to look at nations through a biblical lens. This is kind of like taking an X-ray of them. As mentioned previously, we need to not only learn how to read God's world, but to read God's world in the light of His Word. What delights God's heart about our nation? Are we fulfilling His redemptive plan for our nation?

I think another good question to ask is, "What is stopping God's will from being done in my nation?" Many times, we are rather like a Christian enclave rather than the influencers who control the narratives and life of our land. In fact, for generations we have abdicated our role in stewarding the house of our nation.

I urge thousands and thousands of us to raise up our voices in prayer and action to undo what has been put in place by others who have been fervent in their unrighteous ideologies. While many of us have been devout in our personal devotional lives, we have not been so in praying for the life of our nation, and are now either frustrated or overwhelmed.

I want to encourage you. In the history of nations where there is democratic rule, someone had to be the pioneer. Someone had to say, "Is there not a cause," like David did in fighting Goliath. We learned from David that Goliaths must fall! If we begin the fight and spiritual warfare, we might not finish the battle in our generation, but we will see much good done. The powers of darkness can be broken over a region!

Some years ago, Mike and I went to the city of Medellin, Colombia. Medellin was once a dark place ruled by an evil drug lord named Pablo Escobar. His kingdom looked impenetrable. He had guns, money, and influence. He was the strongman.

However, satan had mistakenly ruled out all the Christian intercessors of the city! They prayer-walked the city and cried out to God over and over. They fasted and prayed and refused to give this beautiful city over to the strongman of violence ruling through

Escobar. Then one day, the US military entered that city and took out that drug lord. Today he is gone and the city is flourishing with new development. Prayer works—and it will work in your city too!

Let's pray:

> *Father God, I know You are the God of the impossible. Therefore, my situation, my challenges are not too hard for You! Lord, help my unbelief and use me to have the reputation of someone who really believes that You can change every circumstance and any dire situation in my family or my community or my nation.*
>
> *In Jesus's name.*
>
> *Amen.*

CHAPTER 12

WATCH AND PRAY

DANIEL DESCRIBED THE invisible realm he saw in a vision when he exclaimed:

> *I watched till thrones were put in place, and the Ancient of Days was seated...* (Daniel 7:9 NKJV).[1]

There cannot be two ruling authorities over one geographical region. There will either be ruling powers of God or ruling powers of satan. There is an ongoing battle for authority over a region that won't be finally settled until we intercede or Jesus returns and casts satan and his minions into the lake of fire. We need to pray that God's Kingdom authority will be established over our nations. Of course, regions will not be free once and for all from satan's attacks until

Jesus returns. Each generation needs to watch and pray over their own generation.

You might be thinking, *That sounds like a huge endeavor! How can I, one person, do such a thing? Isn't that scary or dangerous?* No, it isn't, but it does require courage and the knowledge of how to proceed in a biblical, non-presumptive manner.

EVERY PRAY-ER MATTERS

This is my reply to those people who are feeling overwhelmed at this and wonder where they fit into the scheme of things. You are important and strategic in some sector of society and culture. Each person who prays—each "pray-er"—is critically important to this task. There is a sphere of authority that you have that no one can touch like you can. You simply need to determine what that is and do the part that pertains to you. God will raise up thousands of others who will do their part, and the overall job will be done. This reminds me of the old adage: "How do you eat an elephant?" Answer: "One bite at a time."

You ask, "Well, why does it have to be me? Why doesn't God just take care of it? After all, isn't that His role, not mine, to take authority over wickedness?"

Again, going back to our role as enforcers, the answer is that the Lord has given into our hands the job of legislating His will on earth. He has given us the authority and weapons to do this through what we call binding and loosing:

> *Assuredly, I say to you, whatever you bind on earth will be bound in heaven, and whatever you loose on earth will be loosed in heaven. Again I say to you that if two of you agree on earth concerning anything that they ask, it will be done for them by My Father in heaven* (Matthew 18:18-19 NKJV).

Binding (or *deo* in the Greek, "to tie") and *loosing* (or *luo*) were used in legal terminology at the time of Christ. When the courts of His day would decide a case, they would either say, "We bind (or forbid)" or "We loose (or permit as legal) this in Israel." They would decide what was lawful or illegal, forbidden or allowed, in their nation using this same terminology.[2]

Note that Jesus did not say, "Ask Me to bind or loose." He said, "Whatever you bind or loose ("in My name" is a given here) on earth will be done." He said we are to do it in His name. Therefore, it stands to reason that if we do not take our place of authority in intercessory prayer, then wicked laws have every legal right to be put into place.

We need to pray and do. By this I mean we need to bind the powers of darkness that are blinding the eyes of those who make laws in our nations as well as become voices who speak out against sin in every sector of society.

Literally, Jesus told us that whatever we loose in prayer—or permit—will be legal in our nation, and whatever we bind—or declare illegal—in intercession will be illegal. This is the basis upon which we can "convene the court of Heaven" through our intercessory prayers and legislate in the heavens certain laws of our nations. Dutch Sheets sums it up nicely in his book *Intercessory Prayer:*

> Although Jesus fully accomplished the task of breaking the authority of Satan and voiding his legal hold upon the human race, someone on earth must represent Him in that victory and enforce it.[3]

NOTES

1. There are some medieval-era theologians, such as Pseudo-Dionysius in the fourth or fifth century, who propose that the thrones mentioned in this Daniel 7:9 passage refers to the Ezekiel 1:15-21 beings. These celestial beings are awesome in their powers and could be the "authorities" put in place over nations.

2. For more on this subject, please see my explanation in *Possessing the Gates of the Enemy*, 104-110.

3.   Dutch Sheets, *Intercessory Prayer: How God Can Use Your Prayers to Move Heaven and Earth* (Ventura, CA: Regal Books, 1996), 57.

REFLECTIONS ON WATCH AND PRAY

Every believer on earth has a purpose from God. When we are born again, the call to "steward our garden" comes with it. We are enforcers of God's will on earth.

Just as Adam and Eve were assigned over the Garden of Eden, we are given jurisdiction over the nation in which we live.

I have always said that the news is the Christian's report card. The headlines show us how good of a job we are doing as God's ekklesia; His church. We must watch and pray.

Of course, we cannot pray over everything. There are certain aspects of our society that God will let us know are our responsibility.

How will we know? We will receive a burden. For instance, you may have a child, grandchild, or nieces and nephews, who need to feel safe while at school. Acquaint yourself with their school, what is being taught, and the teachers' names. Become an intercessor for the education mountain by watching and praying.

We only have to read the headlines to know schools need prayer for protection. Meet other mothers and fathers and form a prayer group. You can keep drugs away from the schools through intercession.

If you are a pastor, adopt the businesses in your proximity. Assign chaplains who will personally meet the store owners. I recently met a man named Tony who is a business chaplain. He goes and prays at the stores and for their employees in his assigned area.

If your city has a problem with thieves, pray and bind and loose the spirit of robbery. Pray the fear of the Lord will fall on anyone who is trying to steal in that area. Ask God to send laborers to them to preach the gospel.

These are only a few ways you can watch and pray—and I believe the Holy Spirit will reveal to you what you can do!

Let's pray:

> *Father God, I want to be part of stewarding my nation. Show me my assignment so*

I can enforce Your will on earth as it is in Heaven.

In Jesus's name.

Amen.

CHAPTER 13

BIND AND LOOSE

HOW DO WE know what to bind and loose? God reveals His will in His Word. By studying the Bible, we know what does not line up with His will, and then we develop a prayer strategy to "legislate" His will, or bring our world into alignment with His Word.

When a general goes to war, he prepares a plan. To develop this plan, he needs to know the topography of the land, where the battle will take place, the weapons the enemy has in their arsenal, and even the way the opposing general thinks. He does this through gathering intelligence.

It is no different when we go to fight a spiritual battle against all the strategies that satan has put in place against our nations. We must gather spiritual intelligence and then plan for how we will pray. My friend George Otis Jr., who created the excellent

Transformation series, has coined the phrase for this type of plan development. He calls it spiritual mapping. Spiritual mapping, previously discussed, provides an X-ray of what is happening in the invisible realm so we know how to pray effectively.[1]

We must study the strongholds or illegal places of our nations and put together an intercessory plan to legislate God's will into every sector of society. For too long we have been ignorant of satan's devices (see 2 Corinthians 2:11).

How do we develop a spiritual map or prayer strategy for a specific sector of society? To start with, the following are some good questions to research and find answers:

1. Who were the founders of your city?
2. What did they believe?
3. Were their beliefs biblically based?
4. How did their actions affect the society in which you live?
5. If the founders established your city on righteous truth, did this change over the years and who changed it?
6. How has this affected the thinking of your society?

7. What does your society believe and teach through sectors such as education, media, and other channels of communication?

8. What strongholds have developed as a result of this wrong thinking, laws, or actions?

I am going to illustrate three areas as examples for prayer that need serious legislating in the heavens. They were chosen because of their particular influence on nations and their cultures. Each is a mind-molder in some way and key to renewing the hearts and worldviews of our nations.

EDUCATION

Let's put education in the context of teaching nations. This is how I would do this for the American education system, starting with answering the eight questions presented:

1. The founders were godly believers who taught from righteous educational textbooks such as *The New England Primer.*

2. Their beliefs were that we should teach our children based on Scripture.

3. Their beliefs were biblically based.

4. As long as the original methods of education were in place, the nation and its children prospered.

5. Education took a turn away from God beginning in a visible way in 1933, with the Humanist Manifesto and the change in teaching philosophy presented through the "Father of Modern American Education," John Dewey.

6. Every sector of society has been influenced through humanist doctrine.

7. Educators in general have been taught "situation ethics," the nonethical approach that has led to a moral breakdown in our society.

8. Strongholds of humanism (remember, the humanist believes that the universe is self-existing and not created) have now permeated film, television, art, science, architecture, and all teaching of the liberal arts in colleges and universities.

How do we, on a practical level, begin to "demolish" the stronghold of humanism in our educational system?[2]

1. Be informed. Know what is being taught to students on every level in the schools in your area.

2. Obtain a roster of teachers, look at the curriculum being taught, and find out what the teaching philosophy of the school system is.

3. Go to the library and see what reading material is provided for students.

4. Find an interested group of Christian students and encourage them to form a prayer group on campus. Get as close as you can yourself to the campus and pray. Intercede for God to bring others across your path to join you in prayer.

5. Like Daniel, repent for the sins of the school that your children attend or that your tax money funds (see Daniel 9:8-15).

6. Ask God if you should fast. I suggest doing so.[3]

List the points in the Humanist Manifestos I, II, and III, and ask God to reverse these strategies that have been put in place in your schools. A few of these are:

- The teaching of evolution
- The belief that God is not a prayer-hearing God
- The endorsement of sexual promiscuity

Last, but certainly not least, fast and pray for God to send a mighty revival among the students.

This is only a partial list. Be led of the Lord in your praying, and He will fill in the other specifics that pertain more directly to your area.

ARCHITECTURE

While teaching in a church in Phoenix, Arizona, I shared about the Humanist Manifesto and the devastating spiritual results it has had in our school systems. During that time, I also had a revelation that the Lord would use the graduates of the various colleges, such as the school of music, architecture, etc., to return to their campuses to pray and intercede for God to bring revival to those schools. Then, through their legislating the will of God in these schools, God would free the minds of the students to be open to learn biblical truth, even to hunger and search for it.

There is a saying, "From the roots grow the shoots." What is planted through a life affects the particular sphere that we influence. I believe that Frank Lloyd

Wright's unholy roots affected the school of architecture he founded, which closed in 2020.[4]

In the Bible, Nimrod was a city builder who did so unrighteously. Israel needed to repent of his unrighteousness to get back into favor with God. We need to repent of past sins and pray that God will release righteousness into the teaching of architecture today.

THE ENTERTAINMENT INDUSTRY

There can be no doubt that this industry can be a major mind-molder for either good or evil. Media is, without a doubt, one of the most important influencers of culture around the world. Much prayer has saturated Hollywood from groups such as the Hollywood Transformation Group. I have personally been involved in prayer gatherings at major Hollywood studios. For years, there has been a systematic plan by the homosexual community to infiltrate Hollywood.

It is sobering to say that there are nations today where pastors can be jailed if they openly speak out against homosexuality from the pulpit. However, we must be willing to do just that, even if it means going to jail.

We need to intercede for Hollywood and the homosexual community because homosexuality has become intertwined with the arts on every level. The

Lord wants to touch those who are stars in the eyes of the world so they will have a righteous influence. Intercession must be made on behalf of those in media and communication because what goes across the airways touches millions of people the world over. It affects what cultures and societies think, wear, act, and feel.

At one time the church had godly sway over the movie-making industry. There was even a production code that was strengthened and fortified by the Catholic Legion of Decency, which designated "indecent" films Catholics should boycott. The church has lost its voice.

There cannot be a more critical area for intercessors to focus on in prayer than Hollywood and the media. We also need to intercede for the Christians who are working diligently to change this area of influence.

Many nations of the world have their own film industries, and there is a great need to spiritually map their roots and develop prayer strategies to take dominion in the heavenlies over these molders of society. We all want to see the will of God done on earth as it is in Heaven, and targeting these areas is one way to see it happen.

As stated previously, targeted intercession will unleash revival, awakening, and reformation. And I believe God is raising up a powerful army of intercessors of all ages who will give their lives to pray for God to change the places where they live into holy habitations of peace, righteousness, and joy. Will you be one of them?

NOTES

1. George Otis Jr.'s material can be obtained through his ministry, The Sentinel Group. His book *Informed Intercession: Transforming Your Community Through Spiritual Mapping and Strategic Prayer* (Ventura, CA: Renew, 1999) is an excellent manual on how to spiritually map an area.

2. It should be understood that you must not be involved in any known sin yourself when you begin this kind of praying. Do not attempt it if you are, because you will open yourself up to spiritual attack. For more information on this, see my book *Possessing the Gates of the Enemy,* particularly Chapter 3, "The Clean Heart Principle."

3. For more information on fasting, there are twenty-one references to it in *Possessing the Gates of the Enemy.*

4. Oscar Holland, "Frank Lloyd Wright's architecture school to close after 88 years," CNN, January 30, 2020; https://www.cnn.com/style/article/frank-lloyd-wright-architecture-school-close/index.html; accessed July 12, 2023.

REFLECTIONS ON BIND AND LOOSE

In this chapter we looked deeper into invading the enemy's stronghold through learning the biblical principle of using binding and loosing to develop a battle plan to reform our nations.

We looked into the subject of spiritual mapping, a term coined by my friend George Otis Jr., which helps us pray with informed intercession. We looked deeper still into this with key strategies and questions we need to answer in order to know what to legislate or bind and loose to change a city.

Every city has a beginning. I know most people feel, other than knowing history, it makes no spiritual difference to study one's city. However, this totally ignores the spiritual aspects of the city. Every city has a culture that was created by events in its history. Not only is there a physical culture, but in the second heaven, where the powers of darkness function over a nation, there are strongmen who are real and exist and have the right, through sin, to rule over an area. We will study more of that later.

It is sad to me how many people complain about sectors/mountains of society, without being willing to learn how to pray and intercede to see change in those areas. One of the primary mind-molders of society is the entertainment industry. However, if we really adhere to the biblical mandate that anything is possible to those who believe, then we must take on the giants that have been formed through the sin of the entertainment industry.

There are ministries in Hollywood who have jumped into the front lines of the battle to bind and loose through 24/7 worship and prayer and are being quite effective at doing so. One of these ministries is Radiance International, headed by Jonathan and Sharon Ngai. They began interceding at the old CBS Studios where *I Love Lucy* was filmed. Then they migrated to Sunset Boulevard and pounded hell in West Hollywood. Their prayers availed much as they interceded against the Hustler Club across the street until it closed down. Their building itself was a former porn studio they prayed through and redeemed for God's Kingdom purposes.

Now, Radiance International is taking territory right around the corner from Hollywood Boulevard and the Chinese Theater where "red carpet" movie premiers are held. This ministry includes experts at binding and loosing and clearing the heavens through worship. One of the wonderful effects of all this intercession is that actors and actresses, people in the movie industry, scriptwriters, and others in the entertainment industry are being wonderfully impacted and becoming salt and light in their areas of influence.

In the Education sector, Dr. Len Munsil, President of Arizona Christian University in Phoenix, is committed to instilling godly value systems within the city, seeing the reformation of society at every level. My friends, Hal and Cheryl Sacks, of Bridgebuilders International Ministries, are partnering with them through intercessory prayer and are seeing some wonderful impact on the future reformers of the school. The stronghold of humanism is going to come down through intercessory ministries like theirs.

Architecture, in particular, reflects the soul of the designer. Some structures need to be redeemed, while others need to be renamed. I have known intercessors who prayed and say areas were redeemed and renamed! One is my friend Lou Engle, whose prayer group in Pasadena, California, prayed over an area with a name related to the devil, and saw it given a new, redemptive name.

I encourage you to adopt a mountain of society for intercession. There are many areas that do not have many people invading the enemy's strongholds. I pray that you will ask the Lord which one you are to stand in the gap for to see God's will be done.

Let's pray:

> *Open my eyes and heart, Lord, to see the enemy's strongholds in my city. Show me the idolatrous reasons why and instruct me in how to pray so that every stronghold is removed!*
>
> *In Jesus's name.*
>
> *Amen.*

PART SIX

REVIVAL AND REFORMATION

CHAPTER 14

JESUS PEOPLE

EVERY SEASON HAS a new emphasis the Lord will give to His people. As I have traveled around the world, whether I am in Asia or Africa or Australia, I am hearing the title of Part Six—Revival and Reformation—pouring out in sermons and in private conversations. The gist is that we now realize it is not enough to have a revival. We need to see a reformation come out of the revival. While there is no new truth, biblically, there is restored truth. This restored truth of revival and reformation is especially important in order for us to fulfill the Great Commission and see the nations of the earth discipled and taught of the Lord.

What is revival?

The word *revival* comes from the Latin word *revivere*, meaning to live, to return to consciousness, to reawaken or a renewal of

> fervour. ...So wrote G.J. Morgan in *Cataracts of Revival.*
>
> The Greek word for revival is anazopureo, which means to stir up or rekindle a fire which is slowly dying, to keep in full flame. It is used metaphorically when the apostle Paul wrote to Timothy, "...Stir up the gift of God which is in you..." (2 Timothy 1:6).[1]

Biblical reform means to return to a biblical worldview. Basically, it is the premise that God is the Creator of the world, and so the principles, rules, and the revealed word of God need to be obeyed.

I especially love the theme of this chapter. Many prophetic voices are prophesying a great harvest of the earth is beginning. Some are even saying this could well be the end-time harvest before the Lord's return. I am aware that many generations have felt they were the last and the Lord would come back in their lifetime. This isn't necessarily a bad thing. This longing for the Lord's imminent return presses us to reach the lost and reform our nations back to biblical truth.

The message of revival is very dear and close to my heart. My preacher daddy was fervent for revival. He was a church planter for the Southern Baptists, and everywhere he went he showed the love of God to the lost.

My daddy, the Reverend Albert S. Johnson, went to be with the Lord suddenly. He had a massive heart attack and was gone at the age of 49. One day my sister and I were talking to him on the phone, and the next day he was in Heaven. Mike was my boyfriend then, and he drove me from San Antonio, Texas, to pick up his "effects" in San Marcos, Texas. Daddy's Bible was there, and the ribbon in his Bible was marked to Psalm 85:6 (NKJV):

> *Will You not revive us again, that Your people may rejoice in You?*

There was one sermon in his Bible. It was my daddy's notes on revival. Even to the last, he had revival on his heart.

We have spent a whole book talking about reformation. In this chapter, we look at revivals and the impact they have made on society. Then, in the last chapter of this book, we will connect awakenings, reformation, and transformation. Transformation is the lasting fruit of a regional and worldwide awakening leading to reformation.

JESUS FREAKS

I lived through what has become known as the Jesus People Movement, as well as what is called the Charismatic Renewal. I am going to write more about the Charismatic Renewal in the last chapter because it was, in my opinion, an awakening, while the Jesus People Movement was more of a revival. I am aware the lines between what is called a revival and awakening are at times blurred, but I will focus on the revival aspect of the Jesus People Movement.

While studying at Grand Canyon College from 1969 to 1972, we had a revival that impacted the whole school. At the same time, Arthur Blessitt had made a cross to hang on the wall of "His Place" on Sunset Strip in Hollywood. Arthur had been thrown out of his building on Sunset Strip (or Sunset Boulevard, as it is officially known). On Christmas Day, 1969, in California, Blessitt began the first day of his walk holding a cross. In 2022, he and the cross had covered more than 43,340 miles on foot and more than 2.3 million air miles traveling to 324 countries, island groups and territories.[2]

We were known as "Jesus Freaks" and the "Jesus People," as we called ourselves. On a broad scale, it was known as The Jesus Revolution. Our sign was the index finger pointing to Heaven. We wore Jesus People jewelry, gave the One-Way Jesus sign to each other in restaurants and public places. People, both saved and unsaved, recognized the sign. I will never forget going through a fast-food line. The worker saw my Jesus jewelry and said out loud, "Are you one of those Jesus Freaks?" I proudly replied, "Why yes, I am!"

Basically, we were not ashamed to be called Christians. We were the visible church and loved it!

As a group of college students, we named our particular brand of Jesus People "The God Squad." On Saturday mornings, when we could, we would meet at the school in a room and worship. Someone brought a guitar, and then after that we would pray for God to give us direction on where to go to evangelize. We would pray for a particular neighborhood, and armed with tracts called The Four Spiritual Laws, we would foray out from house to house and ring doorbells. Our endeavors were a roaring success as people in house after house read through our evangelistic tract with us and gave their hearts to the Lord.

Of course we were only a small group, but our actions were multiplied many times over across the nation and the world. New music was written, such as "I Wish We'd All Been Ready" by Larry Norman. We avidly read Hal Lindsey's book *The Late Great Planet Earth,* about the soon return of the Lord. I know a man who got saved just reading the book. We expected Jesus to come at any moment. In fact, I remember one time in college when I felt down because I really thought I might never get married before the Lord returned! Now, going on 50 years of marriage with two children and six grandchildren, I can see that was anguish I could have spared myself!

NOTES

1. Mathew Backholer, *Reformation to Revival* (Britain: ByFaith Media, 2017), 9.
2. Arthur Blessitt Evangelistic Association, https://blessitt.com/fascinating-facts-and-figures/; accessed July 12, 2023.

REFLECTIONS ON JESUS PEOPLE

I have learned a number of prayer principles through the years and the one that is probably nearest and dearest to my heart is this: Intercession ripens the harvest. Many of us have longed for revival and prayed for revival. Others have unsaved loved ones or prodigals they are calling home to the Lord on a regular basis. It seems that some harvests take longer to ripen than others!

Then He said to His disciples, "The harvest truly is plentiful, but the laborers are few. Therefore pray the Lord of the harvest to send out laborers into His harvest" (Matthew 9:37-38 NKJV).

We are seeing signs of revival all around the world, revealing that we are already seeing the answers to our prayers. Here in the US, thousands are being baptized in the Pacific Ocean. University and college campuses are experiencing moves of God, but we need to not only pray for revival but also pray during revival. Then it will turn into an awakening and the reformation of our nations. In Texas where I live, we would say, "We need to stay in for the long haul!" (Translation: For as long as it takes!)

How do we "watch" over for revival? Here are some ways to pray:

1. Pray against sectarianism. In revival, everyone needs to work together.
2. Pray for the fire of God to burn brightly in the hearts of all believers.
3. Pray that satan will not break down communications between leaders.
4. Pray that the harvesters will not grow weary.
5. Ask God to send more laborers into the ripened harvest.

Many past revivals have stopped because of petty jealousies or fights over doctrinal beliefs. Some, such as the Welsh revival under Evan Roberts, seemingly died down, at least in part, because the minister, himself, was exhausted! (We are physical entities, not machines.)

Let's pray:

> *Father God, show me the people who need You as I go about my everyday life. Let me be sensitive to the needs of others to advance Your Kingdom.*
>
> *In Jesus's name.*
>
> *Amen.*

CHAPTER 15

THE JESUS MOVEMENT

THE JESUS MOVEMENT started loosely in the later 1960s and '70s. Magazines from the time, such as *Look* and *Life,* proclaimed such as, "Look out, the Jesus People are coming!" *Time* and *Newsweek* also covered the movement.

During these years, a new newspaper, *The Hollywood Free Press,* started. At its high point, it circulated some 500,000 copies and was full of exciting Jesus People news.

Another distinctive of the movement was an emphasis on returning to the simple life. This movement rose up during what was known in North America as the hippie and beatnik era. Some of the groups, such as the Jesus Forever group in Toronto,

Canada, disdained a strong work ethic because they felt Jesus was returning soon and they needed to spend their time evangelizing. There was also *The Canadian Free Press* newspaper. Of course, a whole book could be written on this subject alone.

During this period, there was the Summer of Love, an event held in 1967 in San Francisco, California. While God was unleashing His power to change the culture, there were other dark forces at work. It is estimated that 100,000 people participated in the Hippie Movement. They wore a particular style of clothing—flowers in the hair and loose, flowing garments. Their lifestyle included free sex, hippie bands, heavy use of hallucinogenic drugs such as LSD, and anti-war protests.

The hippies mainly settled in the Haight-Ashbury district of San Francisco. Other nations, such as Germany's young people, followed their example and held their own Summer of Love events. The Jesus People Revolution ran counter-cultural to the hippie movement. People were set free, many very dramatically, from addictions and the darkness of sin in general.

I believe God sent the Jesus People Revival, among other reasons, to be a force to reform the impact of the Summer of Love to this nation and nations of the earth. The type of drugs being used were very destructive and primarily impacted youth and young adults. I know of a pastor who grew up in Haight-Ashbury and took drugs with his parents from the time he was a young child. When he was saved, he was set completely free from his drug addiction, and God restored his mind. He is a great Bible teacher today and influences a generation of young people.

A number of my friends today are guys who wore their hair really long during the hippie era, not because they were Nazirites! (Nazirites in the Bible made a vow, or were called of God, not to cut their hair. Samson was a Nazirite.) It was simply the style, and even non-hippie people wore their hair longer than the close-cropped style of the previous generation.

This brings up the point that revival movements are usually highly controversial. They are messy, and often stretch the bounds of what the church considers acceptable "church behavior." There have historically been physical manifestations and the breaking of religious norms, such as when Jesus healed on the Sabbath. It is easy to throw about the word *heretic* when something new is happening, but I encourage you not to be too quick to judge.

Sad to say, even though I grew up in a wonderful denomination, because it was non-charismatic I never even knew about some of the greatest revivals on earth. For example, I didn't know about the Azusa

Street Revival, which influenced the Jesus People Movement. Other great moves of God, such the healing revival under John G. Lake, were also completely unknown to me.

True revival also brings unity among believers. I remember this quote from Ed Silvoso about the Argentine Revival: "When the harvest grows so high, one cannot see the fences." An impactful prayer meeting I participated in during the revival in Resistencia in the Chaco province in Northern Argentina was one such fruit of unity. Pastors from many denominations were praying together. All of a sudden, a bass voice rang out. It was the pastor of the Baptist church. The translator quickly shared the interpretation of his significant prayer, "Lord, bless my brother's church more than mine!" He was clearly broken under the power of the Holy Spirit's leading.

When Ed Silvoso and Harvest Evangelism (now Transform Our World), started working in the city, sixty out of seventy of the churches in the city were formed through a church split. Ed's team, led by Dave and Sue Thompson, worked until the churches came together. Then, they all labored together to reach the whole city.

PLAN RESISTENCIA

This story can rightfully go in this chapter as well as the next one on awakening, reformation, and transformation. The Harvest team implemented a brilliant strategy called Plan Resistencia. It involved bringing mayors, judges, businesspeople, artists, etc. of the city to meet with other leaders. An explosion of creative ideas sprang forth from their meetings. Ed raised money to build a water well and a holding tank to meet the resident's physical needs of the city.

At that time, evangelical Christians were considered a sect in the country. They could not serve as the president of the nation and were largely snubbed by politicians in general. Christians there said pastors would come to see the government leaders and wait and wait, until their appointments failed to materialize. (They found out later that the officials had "skipped" out the back door.) However, some thirty years later, the evangelicals have garnered such respect that when a candidate runs for office, they request to come visit the churches during a service.

One pastor, a friend of mine, Reverend Jorge Ledesma, recently built an18,000-seat building and paid cash for the facility. The means he used to equip the facility were certainly reformational in thinking. For instance, buying that many chairs would be very expensive, so they started their own chair-making factory on the grounds of the church site, made their own seats, and saved a lot of money!

Of course, we can't discount the prayer side of this story. The Christians of Argentina are a praying people.

REFLECTIONS ON THE JESUS MOVEMENT

A movement consists of many people being touched by the gospel. I have been in a number of what certainly would be called great revivals. There is an atmosphere of Heaven that surrounds the meetings when this takes place. It might be said that when God's power so charges a place, no sinner can resist His love, and no believer wants to have any kind of compromise in their lives. It is potent, and it is real.

When revival comes, not one has to question whether or not it has arrived because there are tangible signs. One of the most wonderful signs to me is the great unity that comes into the body of Christ. Instead of me, my, and mine, it becomes ours, and the ekklesia, the church, lives and breathes together. There is simply nothing like it.

As of this writing, I have just returned from Argentina. I was privileged to rub shoulders with such giants as Carlos Annacondia, Claudio and Betty Freidzon, and Omar and Alejandra Cabrera in a previous move of God there. Just saying their names evokes memories of spiritual atmospheres where God's power swept over the lives of tens of thousands of people and the miracles were "Book of Acts" quality. Of course, the best part is the souls being saved.

We only have to turn on the news in our nations today to see that the world needs revival; and for some nations, we need revival again! We need to essentially re-dig our own wells of revival. In some cases, in pioneer areas, there aren't wells to re-dig. We need to move together to see that everyone at all times and in every place has the ability to hear the gospel of the Lord Jesus Christ. No one left out. Period.

I like this chapter because it is aptly called "The Jesus Movement." I know we are going to have to work together to get this right and retain the harvest and move it onto reformation. Oftentimes as I have personally experienced great moves of God, I have had a deep, intense cry to the Lord that goes something like this, "God, please show us how to sustain this! Help my generation to be wise counselors to what is going on without throwing water on the fire and shutting it down!"

When Mike and I were in Argentina recently, I asked Carlos Annacondia if he was persecuted when he began to hold large, outdoor meetings with a focus on casting out demons. "!Si," he said, "Mucho!" He went on to explain that pastors' groups actually said he was the anti-Christ and prayed he would never be able to come to their city. "That didn't work!" (Today he is celebrated as having led thousands and thousands to the Lord. It is said that some cities were demon possessed before Annacondia came to town and made a drastic, eternal difference in the lives of many lost souls.)

One of those cities was Resistencia. In a team effort, Ed Silvoso, my dear friend, had put together a masterful plan to reach a whole city with the gospel. It went beyond revival to reformation and transformation. This city was so full of witchcraft and idolatry that they did their own re-digging of their own wells when Pastor Jorge Ledesma and Ed Silvoso together visited every home in the city in a day. The results were powerful!

Why don't we take a moment and pray together right now for a move of God and for our part in it?

Let's pray:

Lord, You know that I want to be on the front lines of all You are doing on earth.

Use me, Father God, to be a help, not a hinderance. Show me how to encourage revival. Open the former wells of the moves of God in my nation and reveal where to dig new ones!

In Jesus's name.

Amen.

CHAPTER 16

RESISTENCIA

WHEN I FIRST went to Resistencia, my job was to teach on spiritual warfare and pray over the strongholds of the city. At that time, the city was, spiritually speaking, a dark, dark area.

I will never forget the night Dave Thompson, I, Doris Wagner, Victor Lorenzo, and a few others went at midnight to pray in the plaza. Argentina at that time was in a terrible period of hyper-inflation. The streets were full of potholes, as were the sidewalks. However, Victor felt the powers of darkness were strongest at midnight. So of course, that is when we went!

We discovered panels placed in the park clearly showing both the visible and the invisible realms (see Romans 1:20). One side of the panel showed a peaceful scene of farmers and fish in a river, and the other side was very dark with images of Kurupi, a very wicked sexual demon, and San la Muerte, the goddess of the dead. Kurupi had a large male organ and was responsible for all kinds of sexual mischief. San la Muerte was worshiped so people would have a good death.

After much prayer, we went back to pray at these panels to pull down the strongholds. It was a powerful time of prayer. What happened after these powers were dealt with? There were spikes in church growth, which meant a large number of people were saved. The darkness or veil that had been over the eyes of the lost was torn down, and the glorious light of the gospel was spread from person to person.

At the end of a large outdoor campaign, where evangelists such as Carlos Annacondia, the Reverend Omar Cabrera Sr., Ed Silvoso, and I preached, the power and glory of God fell! Many miracles broke out and hundreds were saved and received deliverance from demonic powers.

One night, at the suggestion of Doris Wagner (widow of Peter Wagner and my traveling and ministry partner), the team placed a large, empty metal oil drum in the vicinity for people to throw in their witchcraft amulets, potions, fetishes, and the like to burn. This is a biblical practice:

> *Also, many of those who had practiced magic brought their books together and*

burned them in the sight of all. And they counted up the value of them, and it totaled fifty thousand pieces of silver (Acts 19:19 NKJV).

As the witchcraft items burned, screams pierced the air as the people who had been connected to the objects manifested demons. There were teams spread throughout the crowd who gathered the oppressed and took them to the deliverance tent behind the platform.

One of the people who had come to help from a church in the US, where they weren't used to seeing such things, scoffed at people believing that the potions could hurt anyone. He found one of the bottles that had not burned and started putting the liquid on his neck mockingly. It was not very long until he had to be rushed to the hospital as his brain was swelling!

Prayer and spiritual warfare were keys to the harvest. The intercessors would crawl under the high platforms and cry out to God. At times, when the anointing seemed to be waning as I preached, I would stomp on the wooden platform. That was the sign for the intercessors to rev up their praying. Unseen to the eyes of the crowd, there was a spiritual nuclear power plant underneath that platform. I could literally feel the vibration of their cries under my feet as they poured themselves out before the Lord.

One night as I preached, God gave me a prophetic word that there was a Macumba priest far out in the crowd in a big open field. There were thousands upon thousands there that night and I couldn't see anything in particular. However, I was later told that the word was true!

There was, indeed, a Macumba priest who had set up a portable altar, with lit candles, and was throwing some kind of substance into the wind, all the while muttering spells.

The word the Lord gave me that night was this, "There is someone here tonight trying to curse the meeting. It's not working!" The observer who reported to us said, "At that point, the priest blew out his candles and packed them away, along with his portable altar, and went home."

During the worship service, the favorite song for the healing service was "The Man from Galilee Is Passing Your Way!" The crowd pulled out white handkerchiefs and twirled them around. What a sight that was, as thousands upon thousands of those handkerchiefs swirled through the night air!

And after that, the miracles! Miracles of every kind! My favorite was when I was praying for the sick and I saw a small child lifted up over people's heads and passed from hand to hand to the platform. She looked to be around five years old. The little one stood on her feet and gazed around in wonder and started walking back and forth across the platform. People were hugging each other and crying. Everyone was speaking so fast in Spanish that I couldn't understand what they were saying.

Then, a woman came to the platform who appeared to be around sixty. She was crying—hard! At last, Mike and I received the testimony that the woman was the little one's abuela, or grandmother. Abuela had told her grandchild that when they went to the meeting that night, the Man from Galilee would heal her. It seems she had been paralyzed and wore a big body brace. When God gave me the word that someone in the crowd could not walk, and to stand up and walk in the name of Jesus, she stood up and did just that! What a great rejoicing took place at the testimony.

There were many other miracles taking place also. The metal plate in a man's head turned to bone. A little girl's crossed eyes completely straightened to normal. A man's knife wound was completely healed.

Many people were saved during Plan Resistencia. The pastors brought water troughs, filled them using hoses, and held an outdoor baptism service.

This Part Six is titled "Revival to Reformation," so what were some of the changes seen in the city and Chaco province?

- As mentioned earlier, the influence of the church on public affairs changed 180 degrees from 1990, with inroads to city hall especially, and has continued to grow throughout the years.

- There are many Christians occupying local, city, and provincial posts.

- On the recent national abortion vote, six of the seven Chaco delegates voted pro-life (although a pro-abortion bill was passed in the congressional assembly).

- The Director of Public Health for the Province of Chaco is a born-again believer who began to dream of transformation for her city and province as a teenager when she heard Ed Silvoso, me, and others during the Plan Resistencia.

- The current mayor of the city has enacted an open-door policy to the influence of evangelical leaders.

- Transform Our World has raised up young marketplace entrepreneurs, as well as government leaders, through their Christian Chamber of Commerce.[1]

NOTE

1. Taken from notes received by email from David Thompson, vice-president of Transform Our World, March 1, 2021.

REFLECTIONS ON RESISTENCIA

For those who know Spanish, you realize its very name means resistance! Is it possible for your city to change? Yes! When you understand that we need to marry revival with reformation, then the saved souls from the revivals will be sent as laborers into the harvest fields of every part of society. Lance Wallnau, my dear friend, calls them "mountains" and I like to call them that too.

There are two parts of mobilization when we work to reach a whole city. It is our dream for lasting transformation after the revival and reformation. First, we pray and then we act. One might call this prayer activism, mentioned previously. This is when we pull down the strongholds (see *Possessing the Gates of the*

Enemy) and then we send God's people into action into the mountains.

Ed Silvoso designed the transformation plan for Resistencia, and my job, along with Doris Wagner, was to kick out the demonic forces or territorial spirits that were embedded in the city. When dealing with the strongman, it is important to get as many people in the city walking in freedom as possible. This ensures that they don't return to their old behaviors, which permitted the powers of darkness to rule over their city.

As mentioned in this chapter, this was done through having an open-air burning of witchcraft items. The amulets they wore tied them to the demonic structures and empowered the dark forces. One of these was San La Muerte or the spirit of death. Others are Gauchito Gil, which has altars at the borders at many cities and is worshipped for good luck and protection. Some Argentines wear red bracelets around their wrists, and tie red ribbons to the back of their cars representing blood red sacrifices.

Luke 10 is very specific in biblical instruction, showing the correlation between the pulling down of satan's power and many people in a region receiving deliverance:

> *Then the seventy returned with joy, saying, "Lord, even the demons are subject to us*

*in Your name." And He said to them, "I
saw Satan fall like lightning from heaven"*
(Luke 10:17-18 NKJV).

The famous Argentine evangelist Carlos
Annacondia said, "We catch fish, and if we don't clean
them, they stink!" To help you if you need freedom, I
wrote a whole chapter on self deliverance in my book
Deliver Us From Evil.

Jesus Himself put the casting out of demons first
in the list of signs that should follow believers in the
Great Commission. In Mark 16, He says:

*And these signs will follow those who
believe: In My name they will cast out
demons; they will speak with new tongues*
(Mark 16:17 NKJV).

It is really, really important that every believer
understands how to cast out demons. When we go to
reach out to cities, we must make sure that we have no
open doors to satan's attack to backlash against us. I
have personally been through deliverance, and I think
it is good for every believer to receive both inner healing—deep forgiveness and healing from our past—
as well as to expel any demonic beings that were let
in during various traumas. Sometimes a person can

have a spirit of trauma that can open the door to other demons such as the spirit of suicide and death.

Let's pray together!

> *Father God, I want You to use me to full capacity. Show me any open doors in my life where I need inner healing and deliverance. I want a clean heart so You can use me to reach lost souls and even whole cities.*
>
> *In Jesus's name.*
>
> *Amen.*

CHAPTER 17

HOLY SPIRIT POWER

MANY CHRISTIANS HAVE heard or read about the 1904 Welsh Revival under Evan Roberts. I had the privilege, along with my friend Kathryn VanSinderen, to go on a trip to Wales, along with the great revival historian, Michael Marcel. Michael has identified hundreds of wells of revival where revivals have taken place in the United Kingdom.[1] He has personally driven to the sites to do research and invested his own income into giving us the spiritual remembrances of revivals.

In studying the Welsh revival, there were significant meetings taking place prior to God setting Evan Roberts, a former coal miner, on fire for a move of God. There had been a call to prayer for revival starting in 1899 and continuing through 1903. God uses

people in revival, and Roberts was certainly the cata-
lyst God used in such a large way in the Welsh Revival
that he is the one most thought of regarding it.

The roots of Evan Roberts being touched by God
came at a meeting in New Quay, Wales. Pastor Joseph
Jenkins was preaching there in 1903 when a twen-
ty-year-old, Florrie Evans, stood up to testify, saying,
"I love the Lord Jesus Christ with all of my heart!"
Somehow, those words were infused with the power
of the Holy Spirit, and the conviction of sin fell in the
place. It was reported that it was like an electric shock
hit the room.

Two young women from this revival went to testify in Blaenannerch. It was there, in God's providence,
Evan Roberts attended the meeting and cried out,
"God, bend me!" (Meaning, literally, "fold me." He
cried these words out loud while draped over the back
of a wooden divider.) As I stood in that small church
with my friends so many years later, I felt the power of
the Holy Spirit in a massive way. News of this meeting was reported in the *South Wales Daily News:* "The
third great revival was afoot through the nation!" The
other two revivals were the Welsh Methodist Revival
and the 1859 Methodist Revival.

Evan Roberts had a vision that God would save
100,000 through his preaching. He had prayed for
thirteen years to see revival. The Lord often visited

him at 1:00 a.m. and gave him visions, which he would share in his meetings. Hallmarks of the revival were open confession of sin, singing, and giving testimonies. Oh, but the Welsh can sing! Eventually, it is estimated that 100,000 people were saved in the first six weeks of the revival. According to Mathew Backholer in his book *Reformation to Revival,* this was just as Evan Roberts had seen in his vision. J. Edwin Orr stated he believes as many as 250,000 could have been converted during this revival.[2]

However, especially pertinent to this chapter, this revival through him and other preachers of the time led to a wonderful cultural revival. The newspapers in particular were used to spread the news of the move of God. *The Western Daily Mail* and the aforementioned *South Wales Daily News* generated an air of excitement. *The Western Daily Mail* gave extensive coverage to Roberts's meetings in Loughor. The articles were gathered together and published in pamphlets. God wants to use journalists in a big way in the coming revivals around the world. Peter Wagner used to say that any move of God not written about is not remembered. We are indebted to those who have taken their time as publishers of the good news in various forms.

We have so many ways to get the gospel out today! I pray many who are reading this book will be called to write.

One important sociological effect, which was reformational in the culture, was many were convicted of drunkenness in the county of Glamorgan. That led to a nearly a 50 percent reduction of drunken behavior after the revival. This change was critical to alleviate suffering in family structures as the children would have food to eat and other necessities because money did not all go to alcohol consumption.

You may have heard stories about how the revival affected the coal miners. They stopped cursing and the pit ponies in the mines had to be re-trained because they did not recognize their new "clean" commands. Coal miners started their workdays on their knees in prayer. Sports games were affected also with the singing of hymns. Many new hymns were written for the revival, the most popular being "Here Is Love, Vast as the Ocean." That song is still sung in churches in Wales today. I was happy to have it sung for me when I preached in Wales.

A BBC religion article included paragraphs from newspapers at the time of the revival and its effects:

> Houses became decently furnished, women and children became decently clad. ...

Bridges and walls, instead of being covered with obscene remarks, were now covered with lines from Bible and hymn book. The streets echoed with hymns, rather than the drunkard's songs once wont to be heard.[3]

Other things I noted that were reformational were the police were left with virtually nothing to do and the courts were empty. Old debts were paid in full. Revival broke out in a rugby match when 10,000 began singing hymns, and relationships and marriages were healed. Football players joined the street meeting to testify about Christ. Schools were touched by God's power. Basically, the revival touched most, if not all of the sectors of society, and the culture was reformed.

In the Rhondda valley and beyond, God convicted of sin, which eventually led to salvation, which brought about changed lives, sobriety, and restraint. On Christmas Eve in Abercarn, there was not a single summons to court. That had not happened since its formation some fourteen years previously. White gloves were handed out through the mayors of cities in memory of there being no cases the last day of 1904.[4]

I have personally been involved in revivals in various countries of the world. Most of them seem to last only a short while. In the coming revivals, we need to see them go on to cause a reformation in society.

Teaching needs to take place on how to disciple the saved to "go into all the world and make disciples and teach nations." While salvation is eternal, learning how to be change agents in our societies and our need to be involved in Kingdom extending is essential after salvation to see the will of God done on earth as it is in Heaven.

I think we all need to cry out and ask God to bend us to His will 100 percent. My friend, Sergio Scatalingi, a great holiness preacher, says that we cannot think that if we are 98 percent holy we will be where we need to be with God. Two percent poison will still kill us. We need to be 100 percent holy.

It is critical that we look into the subject of prayer awakenings and the coming of revivals and awakenings as we determine to invade the strongholds of the enemy.

We are going to go deeper into these subjects in the final Part Seven titled "Awakening."

NOTES

1. To find out where there are wells of revival in the United Kingdom, go to UKwells.org.
2. Mathew Backholer, *Reformation to Revival* (Britain: ByFaith Media, 2017), 144.
3. Rev. David Collier, quoted in Roy Jenkins, "The Welsh Revival," BBC.co.uk, Long-term

consequences, June 16, 2009, https://www.bbc
.co.uk/religion/religions/christianity/history/
welshrevival_1.shtml (accessed April 5, 2023).

4.   Backholer, *Reformation to Revival,* 145.

REFLECTIONS ON HOLY SPIRIT POWER

Many people know about the revival in Wales under Evan Roberts, but may not have heard about the reformation that took place in the society itself. The miners had a terrible problem with alcohol abuse and drank up all their earnings. Therefore, their children went hungry and without clothes. After the revival, things changed.

I believe the local church is key to the reformation of society. We are called to be disciplers of our nations and to teach nations (Matthew 28:17-20). What does that mean to you, personally? It means you have an important purpose to accomplish while you are here on earth. It means that it will take the whole church or ekklesia to preach the whole gospel to the whole world.

Why am I using the word *ekklesia*? Because Jesus was very particular when He said that the gates of hell would not prevail against the church, and He used the word in the Greek that is *ekklesia*. Because we don't speak Greek, perhaps we don't know the historical context of the powerful word *ekklesia*. The ekklesia was a group of legislators who would be sent into a conquered territory and their job was to "Romanize" the area. So what is being said in this passage? When the ekklesia does its job, our cities should look like Jesus. Poverty should be eliminated. Drive-by shootings and violence should stop. Politicians will govern wisely and will not be corrupt.

There are times when I share about the call to be the ekklesia that people might think these things are impossible. People sometimes comment that politicians have been corrupt since time immemorial. They are really saying, "There are things God can't fix. Sin is greater than the power of the Holy Spirit. Jesus can only save people, but He can't give us the power to change and fix injustices." Of course, no born-again believer would verbalize or believe such things.

There have been a number of great reformers who dared to believe God could change a nation. One of these was the Dutch reformer, Abraham Kuyper, who was a pastor who started reforming The Netherlands by founding a newspaper. He eventually became a righteous Prime Minister. We can stand on the shoulders of such giants of the faith as Kuyper. The precedent he set is a promise to us in our generation.

Salvation Army founders William and Catherine Booth not only raised up an army to save souls, but also provided housing so young women who were traveling by train and got off in London weren't picked off by human traffickers.

I believe that you are reading this today because you are hungry to be a difference-maker. The good news is that God Himself is stirring you through the power of the Holy Spirit. There are today new Evan Roberts, there are new-generation Abraham Kuypers, there are evangelists who win souls and then provide solutions for the lost and dying world!

Let's pray!

> *Father God, I want to fulfill the purpose I was born to do. I am hungry for You and the power of the Holy Spirit to fill me and send me to disciple nations. I give myself fully to this mission while I live and breathe.*
> *In Jesus's name.*
> *Amen.*

PART SEVEN

AWAKENING

CHAPTER 18

AWAKENING—
WIDESPREAD
REVIVAL

NOW WE MOVE into awakenings that lead to reformation and, at last, to a state of transformation.

The lines between what is called a revival and an awakening are, as I mentioned in the previous chapter, fairly blurry. Not all revivals are awakenings, but all spiritual awakenings are the result of revival. An awakening can be defined as a revival that becomes widespread to a region, nation, or even multiple nations. It is when the consuming fire of God burns across widespread areas. A true awakening will often lead to a reformation of societal morals.

Awakenings often begin with one or more people who see the moral depravity of their area or nation and include an intense burden for the salvation of souls. The often-quoted statement is true here: "The world has yet to see what God can do with one man or woman [inclusion of woman is mine] who is wholly consecrated to Him."

The Lord will often supernaturally draw a small group of dedicated friends or even family members together to pray and commit themselves to pursuing God, such as the Holy Club at Oxford.

The Holy Club consisted of just eight members in 1729 and was formed when its members were students at Oxford University. Brothers John and Charles Wesley and George Whitefield were among the most notable, although others in the group also went on to become revivalists. In studying this club, I was interested to note the derision that they suffered simply for wanting to seek God together in a regular way. The name Holy Club was actually a term of derision from their fellow classmates. The other mocking name they were called was methodist, because they had a "method" of reading together and discussing topics about God. They also celebrated communion at their meetings and fasted on Wednesdays and Fridays until 3:00 pm.

In addition to the Holy Club being a term of derision, so was the title of methodists. John Wesley wrote a letter about this name given to mock. He referred to the name given by them by saying, "Some of our neighbors are pleased to compliment us."[1] The name was used by an anonymous author in a pamphlet from 1733 describing Wesley and his group as "The Oxford Methodists."

I believe with all my heart that God is about to stir up many college students on campuses to raise up their own versions of the Holy Club. God will use covenant relationships that He draws together to fervency in praying, fasting, and reaching out to the lost once again. Perhaps you are one of those?

Some peg the start of the British Awakening to the date February 17, 1739, when George Whitefield chose an open field in which to preach to the coal miners in the area because there was no church in the region. (He had been a member of the Holy Club at Oxford with the Wesleys.) There were two hundred in attendance at the first meeting and the next it grew to 2,000!

One author wrote of this area: "Here lived a godless, ferocious race, men who lived beyond the pale of religion or even the law...they were a people apart, a byword for vice and crime."[2]

What happened in that field was truly a move of God. The meetings grew. As many as 20,000 came and they had to move to a larger field in Bristol. This went on for six weeks, and finally Whitefield prevailed to see if John Wesley would take over that work. John and Charles were also preaching in fields at that time. We do not think very much about them doing so, but these were not officially "sanctioned" meetings, and they were opposed for holding them.

It is said that George Whitefield preached 18,000 sermons in his lifetime; 30,000 came to his meetings at the Cambuslang Revival for a communion weekend. It was interesting to find out the taking of communion was part of some of these revivals. This is something that also occurred during the Covid pandemic in the United States, when people started taking daily Holy Communion in their homes.

John Wesley preached 42,000 sermons, which was an average of fifteen per week for fifty-three consecutive years. Wesley was probably the most widely read person of his day, and he felt it his duty after reading a book to comment on it.

These men were consecrated for the work of the Lord, or one could say they were consumed by it. It was noted in some of the books I read that some became too passionate in the times of revival. They never rested and this adversely affected their health.

This may have been the case with Evan Roberts who broke down after preaching so many times. He mostly left the preaching scene after his involvement in the Welsh revival. We must all remember we are human beings, not machines.

I would be completely remiss in this chapter if I did not write a section on probably my favorite aspect of any awakening—that of the role of prayer. Awakening prayer meetings, both pre-awakening and as a result of the awakenings of the prayer, are a foundation stone in their birthing and continued success.

In his book *The Great Prayer Awakening of 1857-58,* Eddie Hyatt writes of the prayer movement that "ended slavery and saved the American Union." It took place in history four years before the US Civil War. Hyatt writes:

> For any revival to be called a Great Awakening, it should have the following three characteristics:
>
> 1. It is an obvious sovereign work of God in that it has arisen apart from any identifiable human plan, strategy or design.
> 2. It is non-sectarian and touches people of all sects and denominations. No one group, or church, can "own" the revival.

3. It is not localized or regional but has an obvious national impact on the nation and its culture.

The Great Prayer Awakening of 1857-58 possessed these characteristics.[3]

J. Edwin Orr is famously quoted, "Whenever God is ready to do something new with His people, He always sets them praying."

One part of this prayer awakening was the moral outrage that grew out of the First Great Awakening. Whereas people had been insensitive, for the most part, to the plight of the slaves, the prayer awakening of this period awakened their hearts to injustice. Abraham Lincoln described the refusal of the founders to acknowledge slavery in the Constitution as being like a man who hides an ugly, cancerous growth until the time comes that it can be eradicated from his body.

NOTES

1. John Wesley, "The Letters of John Wesley, 1732," The Wesley Center Online, http://wesley.nnu.edu/john-wesley/the-letters-of-john-wesley/wesleys-letters-1732; accessed March 5, 2023.

2. John Gillies, "Historical Collections of Accounts of Revival," quoted in Backholer, *Reformation to Revival.*

3.   Eddie Hyatt, *The Great Prayer Awakening*
      (Grapevine, TX: Hyatt International Ministries,
      2019), 4.

REFLECTIONS ON AWAKENING— WIDESPREAD REVIVAL

God is moving today and bringing together groups who are called into covenantal relationships to bring widespread change. These fearless friendships are being supernaturally brought together by the Lord. Their influences are so powerful that they extend the boundaries beyond simply a revival that lasts a short span of time into regional moves of God that release an awakening.

I love the Bible verse from Isaiah 65:8. The first part of the verse simply states that the new wine is found in the cluster. These "cluster anointings" were prevalent in historic moves of God from past revivals. Men such as Steve Hill, John Kilpatrick, and Lindell Cooley were used together to spark the Brownsville

Revival. I believe there were certainly awakening portions to this move of God as people returned to their countries full of fire, like they did when they left the Azusa Street Revival.

Invading the enemy's strongholds takes brave believers. When I studied the history of Westminster Chapel in England, I was amazed to find that the area just up the road from Buckingham Palace was once quite rough. Part of Westminster was once nicknamed "The Devil's Acre" by Charles Dickens due to great poverty, oppressions, and injustice in the area.

The members of the chapel were praying people. They clustered together in prayer and action. They became known for their community work of feeding the poor, and the whole area started to change until it is quite lovely today. An area awakened and was transformed.

You might be one of the first people who band together to pray over a region to believe God for a great awakening. Ask God to connect you with your "cluster" who will pray, preach, and reform the area until God shakes the area and it becomes transformed.

Let's pray:

Lord, I desire to see awakening, reformation, and transformation in my area. Connect me with those in my area of influence who have a heart for the same. Show us how to pray and what to do together to see lasting change! May You be glorified and clearly seen as we walk in unity empowered by the Holy Spirit.

In Jesus's name.

Amen.

CHAPTER 19

A PRAYER AWAKENING

MUCH HAS BEEN written about the prayer awakening under Jeremiah Lanphier. This awakening has also been called the Prayer Revival, also called the Business People's Revival and Businessmen's Revival. It started, as mentioned before, in 1857.

Lanphier had been hired by the Dutch North Church on Fulton Street in Manhattan, New York, to reach out to immigrant families. He was not an evangelist, but rather a businessman. He first tried to hand out gospel tracts and evangelize. Most people were, at best, indifferent to his efforts. At first he was discouraged, but then felt led of the Lord to start a prayer meeting. Of course, history shows that prayer meeting became a prayer awakening.

Let me stop and share a point with you. Great awakenings are sometimes preceded by the potential for great disappointments and discouraging situations. When you are pressing toward God, the roadblocks in your way are only temporary. At times, you might even have fallen flat on your face in your endeavors. When this happens, as John Maxwell has said, "Fail forward."

Jeremiah then had an inspiration, which proved to be from God. He began passing out handbills inviting businessmen to come and pray for the lost during their lunch breaks.

At the first prayer meeting on September 23, 1857, there did not seem to be anything that would forecast the great move of God it precipitated. Six people showed up. Not an auspicious beginning, to say the least!

The next prayer meeting had swelled to twenty-five and the group decided to make it a daily event. In a week, more than one hundred attended. God's timing was perfect, as always, as the week after that, one of the worst economic crisis in American history took place—the Panic of 1857.

This crisis was the spark that caused intense spiritual hunger. Many pastors started opening their churches for prayer, and then the spark became a full-fledged flame. It spread to other cities and the newspapers considered it front-page news.

The meetings were held during the noon hour and had a simple format of taking requests for prayer with no prayer to be more than five minutes long. The power of conviction began to spread to those they prayed for and they began to come under the convicting power of God. Charles Finney, the great evangelist himself, would tell stories about what had happened during the meetings. D.L. Moody as a young man attended prayer meetings like this in Chicago and noted the presence of God. It is fascinating to me how the next generation is deeply impacted to go all out for God by attending prayer gatherings hosted by the generation before them.

For example, in a noon prayer meeting at a church in downtown Kalamazoo, Michigan, the crowd was standing room only. A prayer request was read from a wife asking for prayer for her unsaved husband. Immediately, a man stood to his feet and with tears exclaimed, "I am that man. My wife is a good Christian woman and she must have sent that request. Please pray for me!" He sat down and immediately a man in another part of the house stood to his feet weeping and, as if he had not heard the first man, declared, "That was my wife who sent that request. She is a good Christian woman and I have treated her badly.

Please pray for me!" He sat down and another man stood, also convinced that it was his wife who sent the prayer request, and after him a fourth and fifth with similar confessions.[1]

While I could find little of the personal life of Jeremiah Lanphier prior to his being hired by the North Dutch Reformed Church, simply reading about the persistence, tenacity, and ability to gain a strategy from God on how to structure the prayer meetings during that time tells me volumes about him as a person. I have found one does not simply start something that becomes a prayer awakening that sparks around a million souls coming to Christ without an intimate knowledge of God.

Sean Smith, in his excellent book on revival, *I Am Your Sign,* quotes G.J. Morgan's *Cataracts of Revival* about the preparation of the revivalist:

> God is always preparing His workers in advance; and when the hour is ripe, He brings them upon stage; and men look and wonder upon a career of startling triumph which God had been preparing for a lifetime. God is preparing His revivalists still, so when the opportunity comes He can fit them into their places in a moment, while the world wonders where they came from.[2]

Revivalists are awakeners. They not only win the lost but they awaken the church to its backslidden state and lack of passion and fire. Open confession of sin by believers often breaks open the heavens, and God then begins to pour out His Spirit upon cities and nations.

Sean Smith also quotes Keith Hardman about awakenings:

> Awakenings begin in periods of cultural distortion and great personal stress, when we lose faith in the legitimacy of our norms, the viability of our institutions, and the authority of our leaders in church and state.[3]

In other words, when all around us our nations are falling into disrepair, the young people are disillusioned, people have left God out of the culture, and all seems dark, God comes on the scene. He sends revivalists and awakeners and has already been working behind the scenes to train up reformers who will see that God is preeminent in every aspect (or mountain or society).

Becoming an awakener requires giving 100 percent to God without holding anything back. A revival and awakening without a reformation usually lasts a short span of time—anywhere from a year to a decade. When people are trained with the biblical

understanding that we must also become disciples of our nations, then it lasts and becomes transformation.

It is key here to learn from the testimony of a missionary named Edith Moules. Edith was from Britain and started working as a maid in the home of a pastor. Then she went to Bible school for two terms and left a failure, according to the account in the *Dictionary of African Christian Biography*. She at last took a course on nursing, studied French, and went on a boat to the Belgian Congo in 1927.

She went on to pioneer medical missions among the leper colonies, which was really not something she wanted to do at all because of her fear of contracting the disease. God finally made it clear to her that she should conquer her fear and begin treating the "least of these" who were leprous.

Within a few months of starting their treatments, she had cared for 5,000 of those who were infected. After this, many came to Christ, and there was the need to plant churches in the leper colonies. The results were transformational among the people who had been largely abandoned and left without hope.

I use her life's story to bring home the point that no one is untouchable for those called to proceed from awakening to reformation to transformation. There are many stories of missionaries whose work among various people groups led from their becoming believers, to reformation, and then on to transformation. The Puritans who first came to Massachusetts Bay had an image of an Indian on their seal with the biblical phrase, "Come and help us" (Acts 16:9).

One such Puritan was the Reverend John Eliot, known as the "Apostle to the Indians." Eliot understood that while he could teach the natives the Word of God, they needed to be able to read it in their own language. The problem was, the Algonquin tribe didn't have a written language.

He then undertook to fix this problem himself and developed a written language. It took him twelve years of his life to do so and translate the Bible into the Algonquin. When it was printed, it became the first Bible to be printed on American soil.

Thank God for Wycliff Bible translators and others who carry on this work, as there are, as of this writing, some 3,000 languages with no written records of any type.

William Booth of the Salvation Army made a statement: "Sometimes the need is the call." Rather than needing five poems written on your bedroom wall and four visions to tell you how to start being a change agent, there are things that need to be done for the cause of Christ. Start by cleaning up the trash in a neighborhood or volunteering at a food bank. Find the need and fill it.

There have been times in American history when it was understood that the Bible was the tool God provided as the basis for societal norms and the common good for the underpinnings of the nation. In other words, our founders knew that in order for the nation to be sustained as a republic throughout the centuries, its leaders needed to abide by biblical principles. It was noted that to be a public servant, one must know the Bible. This would be the salt that would keep the savor of the nation and keep it a moral and ethical nation. Its elected officials needed to not only be able and willing to read God's Word, but to read God's world (or nation) in the light of God's Word.

This was so front and center in the history of the US that the congress had a special congressional committee convened to decide whether or not it was quicker to print or import Bibles so that the public schools would not be in danger of a Bible shortage in the classrooms. It was recommended:

> The use of the Bible is so universal and its importance so great...your Committee recommends that Congress will order the Committee of Commerce to import 20,000 Bibles from Holland, Scotland, or elsewhere, into the different ports of the States of the Union.[4]

This could not be enacted because Congress had to be disbanded soon after the fact as the British landed in Philadelphia. Nevertheless, it was reformation that reached the highest levels of government.[5]

I am personally encouraged by the numbers of people who are teaching how to disciple and teach nations in the church today. We are seeing signs here and there of Christians understanding their role to win souls and be reformers by invading the enemy's strongholds with targeted intercession that unleashes revival and awakening.

NOTES

1. Eddie Hyatt, *The Great Prayer Awakening* (Grapevine, TX: Hyatt International Ministries, 2019), 33-34.

2. Sean Smith, *I Am Your Sign* (Shippensburg, PA: Destiny Image, 2011), 20.

3. Keith Hardman, *The Spiritual Awakeners* (Chicago, IL: Moody Press, 1983), 2.

4. "Journal of the Continental Congress" (1907) 8,374, September 11, 1777, quoted in David and Tim Barton's book, *The American Story* (Aledo, TX: Wallbuilders Press, 2020), 187.

5. I am not stating that the United States will be a theocracy during this dispensation. However, the heart and soul of our founders was turned to God. There simply was no separation of church and state.

Rather, it was a separation of an established state church and the state.

REFLECTIONS ON A PRAYER AWAKENING

The role of prayer in awakening is so important that it cannot be stressed enough. It takes great courage to pray when you see very little happening. Prayer shakes the unseen realm and it can take some time until it manifests in the seen realm.

This was certainly the case for Daniel in the Bible. He fasted and prayed, and must have, at times, felt quite alone in his endeavor. After all, he lived and worked under four pagan kings and survived, even being rescued by God from hungry lions. His story always presents a faith challenge to me when I get upset by some kind of setback. The dialogue between an angel and Daniel encourages me not to give up praying because God is always listening to my prayers:

> *Then he said to me, "Do not fear, Daniel,*
> *for from the first day that you set your heart*

> *to understand, and to humble yourself*
> *before your God, your words were heard;*
> *and I have come because of your words"*
> (Daniel 10:12 NKJV).

Note that he was told, *"From the first day that you set your heart to understand, your words were heard."*

Then, the reason the answer was not getting through was revealed!

> *...But the prince of the kingdom of Persia*
> *withstood me twenty-one days; and*
> *behold, Michael, one of the chief princes,*
> *came to help me, for I had been left alone*
> *there with the kings of Persia* (Daniel
> 10:13 NKJV).

Daniel was experiencing high-level spiritual warfare! As he prayed and fasted, there was warfare going on in the heavens. It was not that God had not heard, but there was a huge battle trying to stop him from hearing! It required a battle in the heavens for the answer to get through.

Just as soldiers in the military need to learn strategies and train, so do we as we learn to discern blockages to our having our prayers answered. Many believers get upset at God when their prayers aren't answered.

However, they have not considered that they need to add to their current prayer strategies to see the results.

The following are a few suggestions:

1. Add fasting to your prayers. Remember, Jesus told His disciples that demons sometimes do not come out because it requires prayer and fasting (Matthew 17:21).

2. At times, you need to add more people fasting with you to see the breakthrough. This is where the body of Christ needs to multiply the power of the fast through such ways as fasting chains, where different people, or even churches, tag-team fast to keep pressure against the enemies' strongholds until they break.

3. Develop personal prayer partners. Most of us have problems that are greater than our personal prayers can see the change we need. For example, we have a full-time head of intercession at our ministry, Generals International, and prayer teams that pray at various times during the week.

In addition to this kind of praying, we need Generals of Intercession who mobilize whole networks of people to intercede. We have a 50-state prayer network to pray over national issues.

When God is about to move, there develops a hunger in the hearts of believers to cry out to God for an awakening. Whereas in the past it was hard to get people to gather to pray, suddenly there are lines of people around the block praying. I have seen this happen in Argentina in times of national crisis. Leaders band together to strategize for change.

There is never an awakening without prayer. Maybe you will be one of those who starts a prayer group. Don't be discouraged if you don't see large numbers coming at first. You are front-line warriors who have been chosen to initiate what may later become a blazing furnace of intercessory prayer for your church, business, city, or nation.

Let's pray:

> *Father God, I yield myself to You to be a fire-starter for intercessory prayer. Show me the strategy to pray for an awakening to sweep across my nation.*
> *In Jesus's name.*
> *Amen.*

CHAPTER 20

TRANSFORMATION

I INCLUDE TRANSFORMATION in a book on invading enemy strongholds because I believe that it is possible to teach one generation to "watch over" the next in such a way that a nation can be transformed. I am not talking about a utopian philosophy, but rather that Jesus really meant it when He gave us the commission to make disciples of nations.

A nation discipled and taught of the Lord would be a transformed nation. While we have seen a few nations reach what could be called a state of transformation for a season, it does not seem to stay transformed. However, this should not stop us from working toward that goal. The United States has certainly been a nation discipled and taught by the Lord at various points of our history.

My friend, George Otis Jr., produced the award-winning *Transformation* documentaries that, as of 2018, have been viewed by at least 250 million people in 17 nations. Otis, as noted earlier, says in his history of studying 450 years of revival, transforming revival is the inevitable consequence of fervent, united, and prevailing prayer.[1] (By the way, if you have not watched this video series, I highly recommend that you do. Mike and I worked behind the scenes in a few of the nations highlighted, and we can also vouch for the fervency of the people's prayers.)

George Otis, along with Ed Silvoso, are two of the most notable people who have worked in the area of the transformation of nations. George Otis convened a group of leaders for a roundtable discussion on transformation in the early 2000s. The main topic was to discern how to see a lasting transformation of a nation.

Of course, these steps are tied to revival and awakening. Otis uses the phrase transformational revival. When revival comes, hearts are convicted of sin. God visits and gives correction to His people. This is at times both glorious and terrible.

Once we see a revival and awakening, then it is up to the leaders in the movement to see that there are further steps set in place to reform the nation. This needs to be done in a more intentional manner than we have done in the past.

Awakenings change people's hearts on a large scale, and often the churches grow quite large. If leaders aren't trained in advance for these visitations, then all the church can do is try and put in the necessary programs to teach new believers how to live the Christian life on a daily basis. However, it must go beyond that. We must teach them how to leave the church mountain and go out into all other mountains, become a reformer, and bring societal transformation.

If we do not do this, other religions will begin to come in and take our harvest fields. Intercession ripens the harvest, but the fields fall into decay if we do not become laborers in the fields.

According to George Otis, nearly all Christians readily agree with what God can do on a personal level. Nearly all Christians readily acknowledge that God transforms broken lives through the renewing of the mind. They also accept He works with families (recasting relational dysfunction into models of mutual respect and support) and with churches (replacing forms of godliness with genuine spiritual life and power). However, believers are far less certain when the conversation turns to the transformation of neighborhoods, cities, and regions.[2]

Otis goes on to list community transformation indicators:

1. Political leaders publicly acknowledge their sin and dependence on God.

2. New laws, curricula, and business practices are put into effect.

3. The natural environment is restored to its original, life-nurturing state.

4. Economic conditions improve and lead to a discernible lessening of poverty.

5. There is a marked change in social entertainment and vices as Kingdom values are integrated into the rhythm of daily life.

6. Volunteerism increases as Christians recognize their responsibility to heal and undergird their community.

7. Restored hope and joy leads to a decline in divorce, bankruptcy, and suicide.

8. The spiritual nature of the growing socio-political renewal becomes a hot topic in the secular media.

9. Overwhelmed by the goodness of God, grateful Christians take the embers of revival into surrounding communities and nations.

10. Societal change (transformation/reformation) is a specific result or destination.

> The Holy Spirit will be doing His reviving work long before transformation becomes visible.[3]

Ed Silvoso, my dear friend, as mentioned earlier, is one of the major pioneers in the area of transformation as well. Peter Wagner called him a "world-class missiologist." Ed is not a theoretician but rather a transformation practitioner. He has the ability to work with believers from all walks of life and raise them up to be powerful transformers in their cities and nations. One of the biggest challenges to the ordinary believer today is the belief that they cannot make a difference in their nation. In fact, awakenings, reformations, and transformations begin with ordinary people believing that they can do extraordinary things for God.

I personally do not believe that there are any ordinary Christians—only ones who need to understand that they can make a difference. You can make a difference!

Ed's ministry, Transform Our World, has many success stories of everyday people deciding to make a difference. One that I particularly love involved the transformation of a brothel in the Philippines. This hotel was particularly "successful." The motel chain consisted of eight buildings with 1,600 rooms. It employed 2,000 workers. Each room was used an average of five times a day by 3,000 prostitutes who, in cahoots with the management, "processed" around 15,000 "clients."[4]

The owner of the hotel knew he had to change things. He hired 30 pastors to pray for and minister to the needs of his employees. He built a prayer chapel in every hotel and informed the people as they checked in that prayer was available for them. Couples had to show a marriage certificate in order to check in. The result of their many efforts was that within eighteen months, more than 10,000 clients had come to know the Lord.

To be a reformer/transformer, the leaders of tomorrow need to be taught by the leaders of today how to not only see to their own personal needs but the needs of society as well. In other words, there are systemic issues we need to put our brightest minds to work on. They need to find biblical solutions that will work to eliminate such issues as systemic poverty. They need to develop models of biblical economic systems that provide solutions. The church needs the answers to not only biblical justice issues (for example, fighting human trafficking and stopping abortion), but it needs to find solutions to matters such as food insecurity. It is hard to minister to someone who is hungry. We must first feed them![5]

Now all who believed were together, and had all things in common, and sold their possessions and goods, and divided them among all, as anyone had need (Acts 2:44-45 NKJV).

Nor was there anyone among them who lacked; for all who were possessors of lands or houses sold them, and brought the proceeds of the things that were sold (Acts 4:34 NKJV).

Silvoso writes in his book *Transformation* that in Acts 2:44-46 we see an uncommon reconciliation between the rich and the poor. He goes on to say that people gave extravagantly to the poor, which reflected a dramatic change of attitude on their part—away from using their wealth to dominate and toward using the same to show godly deference. The fact that they fellowshipped daily and in homes shows that it was part of their lifestyle, not a function they participated in sporadically.[6]

This is by no means advocating far-left socialism. Communism and socialism are counterfeit institutions in regard to eradicating systemic poverty.

Believe it or not, there are areas in large cities, even my own Dallas, Texas, where there exists something

called "food deserts." We are to be solution-providers for these desperate needs.

There are exciting works being started, such as organic gardens, like Bonton Farms, right in the middle of poverty. Bonton is the area of Dallas where the Freedmen were settled after slavery ended. However, it was a flood zone, there was no running water, and no public transportation to get to work. Enter Daron Babcock. He left a well-paying job in the financial sector to move into the neighborhood. He was a White guy who passionately loved the poor. He came with his wife and moved into a derelict house. His wife died of cancer, but he stayed on. It was simply horrible for him at times.

He led the local residents to plant organic vegetables. They grew fruit and made preserves. They have added the tending of bees, goats, and chickens. While it is nonprofit, it is also self-sustaining as they have a market that sells their vegetables. They also supply their own farm-to-market restaurant. They hire former felons and give people a chance to start over. As of now, they are planting about 50 acres in produce. Urban gardens feed people, which feeds their souls as well.

Another organization, Habitat for Humanity, has built about 400 or so houses in the area as well. The city of Dallas also built some lovely housing. Sometimes it only takes one person to do something that starts the transformation process. Bonton Farm's visionary, Daron Babcock, says, "It all starts with a seed."

An African organization, Farming God's Way, is doing an incredible job around the world to help eliminate food poverty. This not only feeds people's bodies but provides a renaissance of hope for their souls.

This brings me to share my last point in this book. (Each of these many points are worthy of a book written just about them, and there are some excellent ones!) We are to live a transformational supernatural life. The testimony of a notable miracle has the power to cause individuals, families, and oftentimes whole villages to become transformed. There have been physical healings of someone well known in the community. At other times, angelic protections have been made visible to those who are attempting to take the life of a believer.

The history of world missions is full of God intervening in supernatural ways that opened various cultures' hearts to the gospel. This happens on a broad scale, from medical missions to great authority over the powers of darkness to physical healings to God, as mentioned before, sending angels to protect missionaries.

One of the most impacting missions books I have read is *Before We Kill and Eat You,* subtitled *Tales of*

Faith in the Face of Certain Death, as told to Ruthanne Garlock by the missionary H.B. Garlock.

In the foreword to the book, the great revival broadcaster C.M. Ward says of H.B. Garlock that he was one of the last missionaries who entered the mission field and survived by the power of the Holy Spirit alone. What he experienced in Africa could well be an additional chapter to the book of Acts.

He went on to write that H.B. and his wife, Ruth, "faced the raw power of wickedness, intertribal warfare, cannibalism, the incantations of hell, and the gloom and despair of centuries of superstition."[7]

The Garlocks went to Liberia when that nation was considered the graveyard of missionaries. A good percentage of the missionaries died from malaria within a relatively short time of going on the field. There are so many supernatural stories in this book, I just say you need to read it for yourself! However, I will give a few examples so you will understand my point of transformation.

One chief, after hearing of the claims that Jesus was a healer, said to Garlock:

> White man, you have asked us to give up the religion of our ancestors for a new religion, one that has not been tried by our people. ...We are prepared to consider serving your

God, but before doing so we would like to see a demonstration of this power you talk about. There are many lepers in our village, would you mind healing some of them? ... There are many blind among us. Please heal some of these. And our people are dying every day.[8]

A woman had given birth and not been able to recover, and also had contracted leprosy in the village of Gredeji and died. Instead of burying their dead, they would put the body in a fetish grove and lay it on a refuse heap of skeletons and bodies. She had no heartbeat, but the missionaries had been believing for miracles and decided to take the step of faith and pray for her to be raised from the dead. The missionaries knelt on the dung heap and prayed out loud for all to hear. Ruth Garlock laid hands on the body and rebuked the spirit of death. To the shock of all who watched, the woman's body began to shake violently and was lifted up like she was levitating. The gathered crowd scattered. Suddenly, the shaking ceased, and the formerly dead woman sat up and asked for food.

Three weeks later, H.B. visited the hut of the husband of the woman to find out how she was doing, and he said that she was not there. He inquired as to where she was and was told she was in the fields working. To

H.B.'s astonishment, the woman came up shortly with a huge load of firewood on her head, and on top of that was a stalk of bananas!

As a result, the chief, named Jufuli, who had challenged the missionaries to "heal a few people" renounced fetish worship as did most of the members of his council.

What were the results of them accepting Christ? Of course, the most important one is the eternal one. However, the missionaries were able to persuade the people not to sacrifice their children to idols, to institute good sanitation methods, allow their children to be educated, bring in modern medicine, and deliver the people from being controlled through fetish worship. They also gave up cannibalism and other atrocious practices.

God wants to do these three things throughout the earth: awaken, reform, and transform, which are all connected. I believe we are already in the beginning stages of all three. The Lord is just looking for people He can count on to give their lives on an everyday basis to see these manifest throughout the earth—to see His Kingdom come and His will be done.

It is doable, and it is possible. God is looking for willing hearts and hands to make it happen by invading the enemy's strongholds. You can be an awakener who is led to becoming, on a daily basis, a reformer who brings transformation with your targeted intercession.

Now, be bold, and go do it!

NOTES

1. This was taken from a Q&A session with George Otis from the Christian Union, www.tristatevoice .com.

2. Information sent me directly from George Otis Jr., *Journey to Transformation Beginner's Course* (The Sentinel Group).

3. Ibid.

4. Ed Silvoso, *Transformation* (Ventura, CA: Regal Books, 2007), 112.

5. Note: we want biblical justice as opposed to the term "social justice." Social justice can mean aborting babies and anti-biblical marriage practices, to name a few differences.

6. Silvoso, *Transformation*, 124.

7. H.B. Garlock and Ruthanne Garlock, *Before We Kill and Eat You* (Ventura, CA: Regal Books, 2006), 35.

8. Ibid., 74.

REFLECTIONS ON TRANSFORMATION

It is fitting that the last chapter in this book is titled "Transformation," which aptly describes the last state that can happen after revival, awakening, and reformation. There are many stories of revivals, and some of national awakenings. We know that nations, such as The Netherlands, and Germany, among others, experienced reformation in past seasons. I am sure that, at the time, the leaders could not imagine all their prayers and hard work would not be lasting. However, sadly, history tells a different story.

We need to ask ourselves hard questions. Why is that true? Perhaps we, who have been reformers, assumed that the next generation would, "catch" the principles. Usually what happens is the changes are taken for granted, and people with other ideologies are fervent to undo all the good work in a nation.

It comes down to stewardship. Each generation needs to learn to be watchmen and women to continually train up the next generation. One of the most important areas to steward is education. In the United States, at least, we have had a naive view that teachers were teaching good values. We sent our children to school, and they were indoctrinated while we were unaware. This is starting to change now, and I believe it is changing in other nations as well.

There is an interesting passage of Scripture that I have often pondered:

> *Now these are the nations which the Lord left, that He might test Israel by them, that is, all who had not known any of the wars in Canaan* (Judges 3:1 NKJV).

Until the Lord returns, there will never be a perfect nation that is without sin. Each generation will have their own battles to fight. We need to teach them how to recognize when satan is trying to make inroads into the seven mountains of society. Just like many nations have a standing army, the ekklesia (church) needs one too!

Also, just as armies have specialists, there will be those who are spiritual warfare specialists in each mountain. Satan will continue trying to put his strongman on top of each mountain, and we need to dismantle his work before they become national strongholds.

Transformer watchmen and women are dreamers. They pray with faith to see God's Kingdom come

and His will be done on earth as it is in Heaven. Transformers are also spiritual activists who are biblically literate and answer the call to be voices for God's Kingdom and against satan's plans.

We must both pray and act. Therefore, we need intercessors to see transformation and we need those who go into politics, for instance. For years, the government or political sector has been considered "dirty" by the church. However, with a broad understanding of the role of the ekklesia, mindsets are starting to change. In the past, the church has actually persecuted believers who went into politics, rather than champion them! This is so hard to believe for many of us, but it is still a reality in some Latin American nations. I am glad to have met some valiant pioneers who fought religious and political spirits, both in the church and in their nations. We need to celebrate these people who are working every day to reform and transform their nations. As Ed Silvoso says, "They are learning how to swim in dirty water without getting sick!"

I often dream with my good friends of seeing those like William Wilberforce from Great Britain seize his baton of transformation and invade the enemy's strongholds. If Wilberforce and the Clapham group had not fought the good fight against slavery, that most wicked form of human trafficking would probably still be legal on a large, worldwide scale.

In the United States, I think of Lou Engle, who filled stadiums for twenty years to pray and speak out against abortion. The law that legalized abortion, Roe v. Wade, was overturned on the federal level by our Supreme Court on June 24, 2022. Some states now have no more abortion clinics. I am proud to say that my home state of Texas does not have one abortion clinic, and thousands of babies have been saved since the overturning of Roe v. Wade.

What about you? How are you called to invade spiritual darkness? I believe that each of us was created for a purpose higher than ourselves. We are not meant to just skate along in life, make money, and live for selfish purposes. I encourage you to seek God for your mandate from Him to see transformation in your lifetime.

Let's pray:

> *Father God, I thank You for giving me life. I want to fulfill my purpose on earth. Show me what giants in my nation You are calling me to battle against. I will be faithful to watch and pray and act to see lasting transformation.*
> *In Jesus's name.*
> *Amen.*

ABOUT
CINDY JACOBS

CINDY JACOBS IS a prophet, speaker, teacher, and author with a heart for discipling nations in the areas of prayer and the prophetic. She and Mike, her husband of 48 years, cofounded Generals International in 1985. They also founded the Reformation Prayer Network, which consists of a well-connected, fifty-state coalition of prayer leaders.

At nine years old, the Lord called Cindy when He urged her to read Psalm 2:8 (NKJV): *"Ask of me the nations for your inheritance, and the ends of the world for your possession."* That small seed God planted many years ago has sprouted and grown into an international ministry, taking Cindy to more than 100 nations of the world. She has spoken before hundreds of thousands, including many heads of nations. Some have called her the prophet to the presidents. Cindy helps people walk in the ministry of prophetic intercession, equipping them to pray effectively.

She has been recognized by *Charisma Magazine* as one of their "40 People Who Radically Changed

Our World" and is listed in the Who's Who Among American Women. Cindy has also been recognized among the top 50 leaders in the world who are friends of Israel.

Cindy has written for *Charisma Magazine, Ministry Today*, and *Spirit-Led Woman* and is the author of eight books, including such bestsellers as *Possessing the Gates of the Enemy, The Voice of God*, and *Women Rise Up!* She is a frequent guest on many television shows.

In addition, she is the Chair of the Apostolic Council of Prophetic Elders, which has met together since 1999.

She and her husband, Mike, also convene the Global Prophetic Consultation with invited leaders from more than 65 nations.

She sits on the executive council for Empowered 21 and is an advisor to the boards of Christ for the Nations Bible Institute and Oral Roberts University. In 2019, Cindy joined the Board of Directors of Wagner University.

Cindy earned her Bachelor of Arts degree in Music from Pepperdine University, Malibu, California, and also completed graduate work in Music from Pepperdine. She holds honorary doctorates from Asian Theological Association for her work with unreached people groups, and from Christian International in Santa Rosa Beach, Florida. Cindy also received a third doctorate from Wagner University in Applied Theology in 2018.

Cindy and Mike make their home in Dallas, Texas, where they enjoy spending time with their two children and six grandchildren.

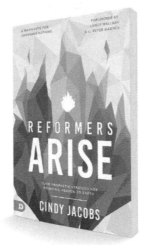

From
Lance Wallnau & Bill Johnson

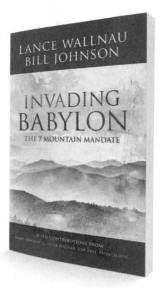

You were transformed to transform your world!

For too long, Christianity has been defined by a false concept of church. As a result, believers have built walls around their lives, keeping culture at a distance.

As Christians have tried to keep culture out of the church, unfortunately, the church has kept itself out of the culture. This was never Jesus' design for the your life!

Before church was established as a place that people "came to," Jesus instituted it as an army that brought transformation to society, starting with salvation and continuing with seven spheres of influence: Church, family, education, government, media, arts, and commerce.

Six revolutionary voices in the modern church deliver Invading Babylon. This essential guide will equip you to:

- Understand your vital role in shaping society.
- Release God's will in your sphere of influence.
- Become an unstoppable citizen in God's Kingdom.

It's your time to arise and be a light in a dark world.

Purchase your copy wherever books are sold

YOUR
Prophetic
C O M M U N I T Y

Sign up for a **FREE** subscription to the Destiny Image digital magazine and get awesome content delivered directly to your inbox!

destinyimage.com/signup

Sign up for Cutting-Edge Messages that Supernaturally Empower You

· Gain valuable insights and guidance based on biblical principles
· Deepen your faith and understanding of God's plan for your life
· Receive regular updates and prophetic messages
· Connect with a community of believers who share your values and beliefs

Experience Fresh Video Content that Reveals Your Prophetic Inheritance

· Receive prophetic messages and insights
· Connect with a powerful tool for spiritual growth and development
· Stay connected and inspired on your faith journey

Listen to Powerful Podcasts that Propel You into God's Presence Every Day

· Deepen your understanding of God's prophetic assignment
· Experience God's revival power throughout your day
· Learn how to grow spiritually in your walk with God

In the Right Hands, This Book Will Change Lives!

Most of the people who need this message will not be looking for this book. To change their lives, you need to **put a copy of this book in their hands.**

Our ministry is constantly seeking methods to find the people who need this anointed message to change their lives. **Will you help us reach these people?**

Extend this ministry by sowing three, five, ten, or *even more* books today and change people's lives for the better! Your generosity will be part of catalyzing the Great Awakening that many have been prophesying and praying for.